The

Handbook

Stuart Morley
BMus(Hons) PG Dip Dip RAM ARAM

Foreword by Ben Elton

Bright Pen

Visit us online at <u>www.authorsonline.co.uk</u>

A Bright Pen Book

Copyright © Stuart Morley 2011

Cover design by Stuart Morley ©

British Library Cataloguing in Publication Data.
A catalogue record for this book is available from the British Library.

ISBN 978 0 7552 1414 3

Authors OnLine Ltd
19 The Cinques
Gamlingay, Sandy
Bedfordshire SG19 3NU
England

This book is also available in e-book format, details of available at www.authorsonline.co.uk

for Lizzie, with love

FOREWORD

I have loved Musical Theatre ever since I was a boy. It's a wonderful medium that can delight and inspire audiences in ways that no other art form can. Of course it wasn't until I got involved in Musical Theatre professionally, both as a writer and director that I began to understand what a hugely challenging and complex business it is. One of the most important roles of all is that of Musical Director. He or she must bring their own creativity to bare while remaining faithful and true to the dramatic intent of the writers and composers. They must be able to integrate the music into the drama so it flows as one. They must be sensitive to the individual talent and potential of the artists with whom they are working (and whom they will often have cast). Above all they must be a strong musical leader who can nurture and inspire both singers and musicians to achieve their very best. And do so eight times a week!

Having worked with Stuart for four years on the London production of "We Will Rock You" I am thrilled that he has put together this handbook that discusses the technical requirements and the processes involved in putting on a show. I hope and believe that it will be a useful aid to all those serious about learning this unique art form.

Ben Elton
Author, Playwright, Director and Comedian

PREFACE

Ever since I travelled down to London in my early teens to see "Joseph and the Amazing Technicolour Dreamcoat" at the London Palladium, I longed to work in the West End. Seeing Mike Dixon conduct the massed vocal and instrumental forces in that magnificent theatre had a profound effect on me, and it is a memory that will stay with me forever. Musical theatre never fails to inspire me, and I feel very fortunate now to be able to work professionally in this exciting business they call *Show-Business*.

I have written this handbook in the hope that it will be a useful aid to all those who want to learn more about what it means to be a Musical Director. In addition to the advice and encouragement from some incredible teachers (Dave H, Mr P, June, Catherine, Greg, Mary, Karen and George, David and Mark) I have learned, and indeed continue to learn, on the job, as there are very few specific resources to help musical directors find their way. In writing this handbook I have drawn on my own experiences, and on the knowledge that has been passed on to me from those who've helped and guided me along the way. I hope that the reader can benefit from the notes that follow, and hopefully start (or continue) their Musical Directing journey armed with a little more knowledge than myself and many others before me had. This handbook is intended for those who are trying their hand at Musical Direction for the first time, or who have some experience of Musical Direction and are keen to broaden their knowledge on the subject. It's not aimed at professional Musical Directors as one would obviously hope they already know what they're doing, although some may choose to have a look just to see if they concur with my methods and fancy a fresh perspective on this unique job.

Looking back to my early days of doing college and amateur dramatic shows, frantically trying to find a trumpet player for the ULOG production of "Princess Ida" and writing out arrangements for ATA Productions at three o'clock in the morning fuelled by the strongest instant coffee a student budget could afford, I think how green I must have looked in those days boldly asking a particular Director "so what is "tech" then?" and sitting in my first ever real production meeting enquiring "what actually does the Designer do?". Luckily I met some kind and understanding people who could have easily laughed in my face, but instead decided to answer my naive questions and point me in the right direction.

The journey from our back room in Hull where my big brother showed me how to write out "If George should come" before heading off to school, to the night when Keith Strachan called to offer me my first professional tour has been exciting, nerve racking, exhausting, inspiring, humbling and financially stretching. It's a journey that I still love to take on a daily basis, and I can only hope that it's one you'll enjoy taking too.

Stuart Morley
December 2011, London

CONTENTS

THE MUSICAL DIRECTOR'S HANDBOOK

The World of Musical Theatre

Welcome to the wonderful world of *Musical Theatre* – a giant melting pot combining performance, lighting, special effects, Musicians, Dancers, Actors, Technicians, Directors, Designers, Choreographers, and of course... the *Musical Director*.

Whether you have found yourself thrown in at the deep end as Musical Director for a school or college production, have gallantly agreed to wield the baton for an amateur or community theatre production, or you are a professional musician who has taken a Musical Director or Assistant Musical Director job for the first time, I hope this handbook will provide you with some tips that will help you along the way, and some notes to ensure that your Musical Director experience is a happy and fulfilling one.

When writing this handbook I have drawn on my own experiences working with amateurs and professionals alike, and have also chatted to numerous other Musical Directors, Directors and Choreographers who are currently working in the theatre industry. My aim is to consolidate some thoughts on the art form that is Musical Direction into a format that can either be read cover to cover, or dipped in and out of as necessary. For those approaching Musical Direction as a beginner, this handbook should be read chronologically and then referred back to, as appropriate, at a later date. More experienced readers will hopefully be able to use the book as a way of confirming that which they already know, and may find some areas they would like to address in their current technique and working practices.

Musicals are a unique combination of music, drama, dance and technical theatre. The role of Musical Director involves working closely with actors, dancers and musicians, so it is important that you build up a knowledge of these different theatrical disciplines in order to fully connect with the people you are working with. This doesn't mean you should race down to your nearest dance class (perish the thought) or read the entire works of Shakespeare, Brecht and Pinter, but it does perhaps mean that you should try to develop a wider appreciation of how dancers and actors work, and an awareness of the separate disciplines and skills that combine to make a Musical.

In the chapters that follow we will explore the various skills that are required of the Musical Director, as well as discussing the roles and responsibilities that the job entails. There are several exercises to help further develop your Musical Director skills, and also some suggestions for further study should you want to delve deeper into this unique art form. For those approaching Musical Direction for the first time there are descriptions of some theatrical terminology which you're likely to encounter, as well as some job descriptions of your Musical Theatre work colleagues.

SO WHAT EXACTLY IS A MUSICAL DIRECTOR?

The Musical Director is the member of the Artistic Team who is responsible for all of the musical elements of a show. Most people recognize the Musical Director as the person who *conducts* the performances, but there is a lot more to it than just waving your arms around in a rather bizarre way! The Musical Director is responsible for teaching the *Score* to the cast, rehearsing the band/orchestra, meeting with the members of the *Creative/Artistic Team* (Director, Choreographer, Designers – Lighting, Sound, Costume and Set) to decide the shape of the show and what format it will take, and ultimately conduct the performances. This will either be done with a baton or from the keyboard (a practice associated with more contemporary shows). When the show is up and running it is the Musical Director's responsibility to maintain the standard of the cast and orchestra, to give notes on the performances, and to call *clean-up* rehearsals as required.

The Musical Director is one of the few members of the Artistic Team who is present both in rehearsals and performance. They have a constant responsibility to the cast, the writers (whether or not they are present during the rehearsal process) and to the Director, Choreographer and Designers, to ensure that the music department is managed effectively and efficiently. It is vital that they are always punctual, prepared (to the best of their ability) and perhaps most importantly that they are seen as someone who is reliable. When the Cast, Musicians and Technical Department look down into the *Orchestra Pit*, or up to the TV monitor relay, it is of paramount importance that they see someone who they can trust, and someone who will help them perform their role to the best of their ability. A wise friend once said that you cannot command respect, you can only earn it. You will only achieve this by being reliable, responsible, well prepared, in control, focused on the show, fair in your decision making, positive and musically solid. There is no place for a Musical Director who is only interested in the so called "power" that comes with the job, or one who is in it to inflate their ego. In one of his famous *Omnibus* broadcasts of 1954, Leonard Bernstein said of the Conductor that "All his efforts, however strenuous or glamorous they may be, [must] be made in the service of the music itself, which after all is the whole reason for the Conductor's existence". It is a big responsibility to direct the music for a show, and it is one that should be undertaken with a clear, open and focused mind.

Being the Musical Director can be an extremely rewarding experience, bringing with it some fantastic highs. The feeling of conducting the final chord on an opening night as the front cloth hits the stage floor is unsurpassed, and the adrenaline rush you feel when you are taken on the journey with an actor while you conduct them through an emotional ballad is like no other. So, if you have decided this is the job for you, keep reading!

Find out more

If you are new to Musical Direction and want to find out more about the journey ahead, why not call Stage Door at the theatre where your favourite show is playing and ask them who the Musical Director is? Then drop them a line and ask if you can have a chat with them over a coffee, and maybe even sit in the pit for a performance to see how it all works. Watching an experienced professional in action is a great way to learn.

More experienced readers may also benefit from watching fellow Musical Directors in action. A lot can be learned from watching others work, no matter what stage your own career is at. There is little place in Musical Theatre for the Musical Director who sits back and rests on his or her laurels!

THE MUSIC DEPARTMENT

Musical Director – The person responsible for ensuring the musical score is taught to the cast and band, and the person responsible for conducting the performances. The Musical Director is effectively the head of the music department in the Theatre. (English abbreviation – MD)

Musical Supervisor – The person who supervises and supports the Musical Director (generally present on larger shows) and normally the person who "sets up the show" (prepares the Vocal Score, liaises the Writers, Designers, Director and Choreographer about the concept). The Musical Supervisor will then act as a consultant, leaving the day-to-day running of the show to the Musical Director.

Rehearsal Pianist – A freelance pianist who is engaged to play for rehearsals/calls (including dance calls and Understudy rehearsals). Depending on the production one rehearsal pianist may be engaged for the whole rehearsal process, or the work may be shared between several pianists. It is not uncommon for the Assistant Musical Director to accompany singing, staging and dance rehearsals.

Assistant Musical Director – Someone who assists the Musical Director in the day-to-day running of the show. The Assistant Musical Director will normally play one of the keyboard parts (chairs) for the performance, and will usually be 1st cover conductor. (English abbreviation – AMD)

SHOW PERSONNEL

Producer(s) – The person (or team of people) who are putting on the show. The Producer sometimes offers artistic input, but essentially they have engaged their Creative Team to make the artistic choices for them. The Producer is generally the person who is financing the production period and also the person who makes most of the money if it is a success! The Producer is also the person who "presents" the show (e.g.: "*Cameron Mackintosh* presents...") and therefore they are essentially "in-charge". In Amateur/Community theatre the Society/Group's committee is effectively the Producer (eg: "*Tunbridge Wells Operatic Society* presents..."), and when a show is produced "in-house" by a Theatre the Theatre Management would be the Producer (e.g.: "*Millfield Theatre* presents...")

CREATIVE TEAM

Director – The Artistic Boss! The Director is in charge of the overall shape of the show and oversees all artistic aspects of the production. They lead the acting rehearsals and "stage" the show, working with the actors on developing their characters as well as directing the movement/blocking in the scenes. It is the Director's job (along with the Designer) to interpret the script and realize the drama on-stage.

Choreographer – The person in charge of the dancing. The Choreographer will conceive the dance routines, and work with the Director on the musical shape and design of the production. They will be responsible for teaching the routines to the Cast (often with the help of an Assistant Choreographer and Dance Captain), and will co-ordinate with the Musical Director/Supervisor to ensure the Choreography marries with the Score.

Designer(s) – The person (or team of people) who work with the Director and Choreographer (and writers if it is a new work) to interpret the script and transform it into stage production. The Designers are not often present in the rehearsal room, but are a vital part of any production. They are responsible for set design, costume design, lighting design and sound design. It is quite common (especially on smaller productions) for the set design and the costume designs to be done by the same person.

# Chapter 1:
What skills should the Musical Director possess?

A CONFIDENT MUSICIAN

Primarily the Musical Director should be someone who is comfortable teaching and rehearsing the score with the cast (either from the piano or aided by a rehearsal pianist), rehearsing the band/orchestra, and ultimately conducting the final performance(s). The Musical Director should therefore be someone who is a confident musical leader, and also a knowledgeable, proficient and versatile musician.

If you are new to Musical Direction and you aren't feeling 100% confident at the moment, please don't panic! Hopefully this handbook can help to iron out any worries and doubts that may be lingering.

A THEATRICAL ALL-ROUNDER

The Musical Director's job involves working with a variety of people from different theatrical disciplines. As well as taking the ensemble vocal rehearsals, they have one-to-one work sessions with the principal actors, are responsible for rehearsing the score with the band/orchestra, work with the technical team (including the sound and lighting department) and form a vital part of the artistic team, which includes the Director, Designers and Choreographer. It is this team which works together to discuss and plan the overall shape of the show.

It is therefore desirable for the Musical Director to have an awareness of as many aspects of theatrical life as possible. That doesn't necessarily mean you need to have "hands-on" experience of the different disciplines (although I think we should all experience at least one street jazz dance class to fully appreciate what dancers go through), but it does mean that the Musical Director should always keep their eyes and ears open in rehearsals so that they can develop an understanding of acting, dance and technical working practices and terminology. This knowledge will be invaluable when entering discussions with the creative and artistic team in production meetings.

Through the following chapters we will explore the various skills required of the Musical Director, and discuss ways to help further develop your knowledge of the inner workings of theatrical life so you feel fully equipped for the task ahead.

THE MUSICAL DIRECTOR UMBRELLA

The title of "Musical Director" is an umbrella term covering several specific roles:

- The **Conductor** - someone who feels confident and technically able to conduct the performances either with a baton, using their hands, or from the keyboard. All Musical Directors should have a solid conducting technique as there are many things to think about when conducting a show and there won't be any time to think about the actual mechanics of conducting. Those who are new to Musical Direction should take time to develop a solid and clear conducting technique before entering the rehearsal room for the first time. More experienced Musical Directors should constantly assess their own technique, either by occasionally filming their performances or by practicing in front of a mirror in order to ensure no bad habits or unnecessary flamboyancies creep in.

- The **Pianist** – someone who can play for vocal and dance rehearsals, and also play as part of the Band if required. The Musical Director will sometimes be asked to adapt the Vocal Score arrangements for a specific production, re-work dance routines and re-arrange music at the keyboard. Keyboard proficiency is therefore invaluable for all Musical Directors.

- The **Singer** – someone who is happy to sing out the harmony lines "loud and proud" during rehearsals. In an ideal world the Musical Director should be comfortable demonstrating the kind of sound and type of phrasing which they want in front of a group, and should also have a good working knowledge of the voice and the different vocal styles and techniques.

- The **Actor** - someone who always has an eye on the drama. The Musical Director should be able to help a singer/actor work on the character development through the songs, and facilitate the use of the music as a tool to move the drama forward.

- The **knowledgeable Musical Director** – someone who has done their homework before rehearsals. They know the music, they know the story, and they know the show. The Musical Director should be someone who's knowledge can be relied on at all times, and someone who can lead the music intelligently and confidently. The musician who has an in-depth knowledge of the "Golden Age of Musical Theatre" but has never listened to any rock music is sure to fail when directing the music for "Tommy"; and the musician who has an intimate knowledge of the works of Jason Robert Brown but is unaware of the classic works of the 1940's and 1950's is destined to fail when they turn up for the first day of rehearsals for "Carousel".

Ideally the Musical Director should have an awareness of dance, and an appreciation of the skills required to dance in Musical Theatre. It is helpful for them to understand certain dance terminology and be sympathetic to the specific demands which are put on show dancers.

PEOPLE SKILLS

In addition to the skills and knowledge mentioned above, it is important for the Musical Director to possess good people skills. The nature of the job means you will sometimes find yourself participating in spirited discussions between the various artistic forces that come together to make the production happen. You will need to make your views heard at such times, whilst exercising an appropriate level of diplomacy.

For example, in the rehearsal room you may be asked to make changes to the score or adapt the music in a way that goes against your own musical judgment. If you are tired or having a bad day there may be the urge to jump up and defensively shout your objections to the equally tired Director or Choreographer. You should avoid a confrontation in front of the cast at all costs. All this will achieve is a messy ego battle that will ultimately undermine the Artistic team in the eyes of the cast. It would be better to whisper your concerns away from the cast, or better still to discuss concerns at the end of the rehearsal once the cast have left the room.

There will also be times when you have to compromise your musical ideal for the good of the show. Remember that a *Musical* is a combination of acting, dancing, singing and many other technical aspects (lighting, sound, visual FX etc.). Always do what is best for the show as a whole, even if this is not your personal musical ideal.

Actor-Muso Shows

There are a number of shows where the Band, Cast and Dancers are one of the same. These are called Actor/Musician Shows (or "actor/muso" for short). In these shows the performers are required to play instruments (often several different ones) as well as acting, dancing and singing. An example of this type of show is the Rock and Roll Musical "Return to the Forbidden Planet" (Bob Carlton, 1989). There are also instances where the Musical Director is required to perform a small cameo role, such as the recent productions of "Chicago" where the band are on-stage and the Conductor interacts with the cast and audience, or "Sister Act" where the Conductor also plays "The Pope" in the final sequence. In the original Broadway production of "Curtains" the Conductor (Sasha) even sang the opening to Act 2!

DEVELOPING YOUR MUSICAL DIRECTOR SKILLS

In the chapters that follow we will explore the various skills required of the Musical Director, and look at ways to develop these skills. We will examine the processes involved in mounting a Musical Production and also discuss the vital role that the Musical Director plays within that process.

Make sure you are equipped for the journey ahead

THE MUSICAL DIRECTOR'S PENCIL CASE

A fully stocked pencil case is a vital part of your Musical Director toolbox, and an essential asset in the rehearsal room. You will find it helpful to have the following items in your pencil case:

- 2B pencils (the softer lead is easier to rub out when things change)
- Pencil sharpener (a blunt pencil is both frustrating and useless!)
- Eraser (Things often change in rehearsals so make sure you always work in pencil, and that you have an eraser to hand to rub things out and change them if necessary)
- Coloured pens/pencils (In case you need to make notes that will stand out, or that are colour coded in either your Score, or in your rehearsal note pad)
- Highlighter(s) (great for marking cue lines in your script or for highlighting things in your score)
- Post it notes – the little ones are particularly useful (handy for marking in cuts and changes – especially where things are frequently changing, as they are easily removed)

Other useful things to have in your Musical Director's bag are:

- Note Pad and Pen (for making rehearsal notes)
- Metronome* (to ensure your tempos are consistent, and to check metronome marks in the rehearsal room. This is especially important in dance rehearsals)
- Dictaphone/Digital Voice Recorder* (to record anything you change, but don't have time to write out fully in the rehearsal room, such as new underscore and dance breaks/instrumentals)
- Manuscript Paper (to note any musical changes you make)
- Stop Watch* (particularly handy when you are working on a new show for timing scene changes or underscoring)

*If you are a Smart Phone user you should be able to download a metronome, stopwatch and Dictaphone/voice memo app. to save you carrying them around with you in your bag. If this is the case it's probably worth carrying a phone charger with you so you're not left stranded if the battery dies.

﷼Chapter 2: **Developing your skills**

PUTTING ON A SHOW

A Musical goes through several key phases before it reaches the performance stage. If the Musical Director is involved on a regular basis with a particular company they may be involved in the early pre-production stages, including selecting the show and deciding on the performance dates. If the Musical Director is appointed after the production company has decided to mount a specific production they are more likely to join at the planning stage, or sometimes as the casting process begins. Each company has it's own way of working and therefore each production process is unique.

However the show is mounted, it will usually go through the following stages before arriving at opening night:

- **Deciding to put on a show** – In the Amateur Dramatic/Community Theatre world the company will often have set times of the year in which they mount a production (e.g. every March and October), therefore there will come a time when the committee will meet to decide what particular show they would like to do. Once they have made their decision they will apply for the performance rights (permission from the publishers) before announcing their choice to the Company. This is normally the point where the Director, Choreographer and Musical Director will be appointed. A similar process will usually follow for School and College productions whereby members of staff will meet to discuss the various options before deciding on a specific show they would like to perform.

  In the professional theatrical world it may be that a particular Producer (or Theatre that produces Musicals "in house") will decide they would like to mount a professional production of a particular Musical. Once the performance rights are secured they will then appoint a Director. At this point they will either ask the Director for suggestions for a Musical Director/Supervisor, Choreographer and

Designer(s), or appoint them all at the same time (depending on the individual Producer's working practices).

- **Planning the Show** – Once the Director, Choreographer, Designer(s) and Musical Director/Supervisor have been appointed they will usually meet to discuss the form the show will take and to plan how to mount the production. This may include discussions about the Characters, the set, the band, the musical shape of the piece and the choreographic style. In order for this meeting to be as productive as possible, it is helpful if the Musical Director has planned ahead – i.e. read the script, looked at the score, checked the size of the orchestration and is familiar with the music.

- **Personal preparation time** – learning the show (see chapter 3)

- **Casting the show** – deciding who will play the different roles, and who will be in the ensemble. This will normally happen directly after the audition process (see chapter 4)

- **Rehearsing the Show** – teaching the score to the cast and band/orchestra (see chapter 5)

- **Performing the Show** – moving from the rehearsal space into the Theatre/performance space to perform the finished production (see chapter 6)

In order to ensure the journey to opening night is as smooth as possible, it is important that you prepare fully for the task ahead. As well as possessing the necessary technical skills required to direct the music for the production, it is vital to spend suitable time preparing the score and doing the relevant background research before the production process begins. It is important that you feel confident in yourself before you walk into the all-important first meeting with the Director, Choreographer and Designer(s).

COOL, CALM AND CONFIDENT

In order for you to feel cool, calm and confident when you introduce yourself as the "Musical Director", we need to make sure that your musical toolbox is packed full with the information, knowledge and skills you need for the task ahead. In the sections that follow we will discuss the process of mounting a production, and examine in greater depth the vital role that the Musical Director plays in that process.

he Specifics

THE CONDUCTOR

It is important for all Musical Directors to possess a solid conducting technique. Although many modern productions (either new shows, or revivals of older classic Musicals) are now led from a combined Piano/Conductor position and less are now conducted with a baton, all shows require an element of conducting.

It is part of the Musical Director's job to lead the cast, band and technical department through a performance. This can only be done well with clear and consistent cueing and conducting.

Clarity is of vital importance. All Musical Directors should take time for self-evaluation, whatever stage their career is at. Less experienced conductors should spend time videoing themselves - then watching back to see if their conducting is clear and consistent. More experienced conductors should do the same, since bad habits such as distortions of the beat patterns, odd facial expressions and unnecessary gesticulations may have gradually developed over time. Mirror practice is also valuable should you not have a video camera to hand.

Beginners should familiarize themselves with all of the basic beat patterns, and practice these until they become second nature.

Many readers will already have a prior knowledge of the different beat patterns so we won't explore these in this chapter. However those who would like a refresher or need to learn the basic beat patterns should refer to Appendix 1.

In addition to knowing the basic beat patterns you need to be able to cue players and singers, set **and hold** a tempo so that is consistent from show to show, conduct *hits* and *buttons, pauses/fermatas, bring-offs* and indicate dynamic changes.

PHYSICALITY & POSTURE

The first thing that the actors and musicians will notice when they look to the conductor for musical leadership is their posture. A good stance will help you look relaxed and authoritative when conducting, whereas a bad posture can give the wrong vibe, making you appear unconnected, disinterested and uncomfortable.

It is vital that the actors and musicians feel they are being *led,* both in rehearsal and in performance (as opposed to having someone "marking time" along with the music). You should therefore take care to ensure that you *look* the part, and that your posture and physicality are conveying the right image to those with whom you are working.

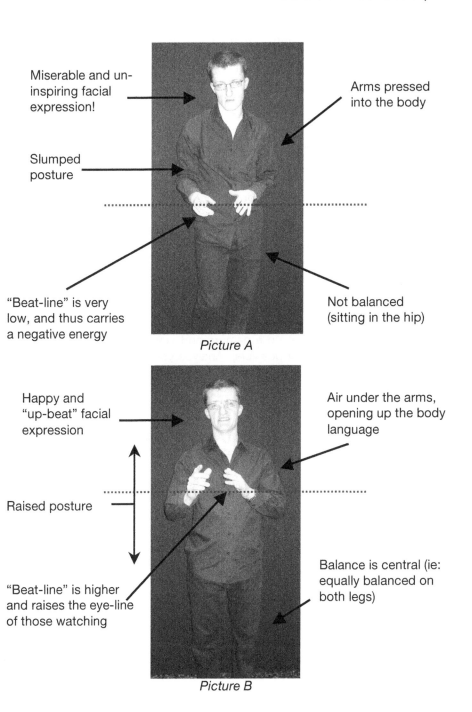

Miserable and un-inspiring facial expression!

Arms pressed into the body

Slumped posture

"Beat-line" is very low, and thus carries a negative energy

Not balanced (sitting in the hip)

Picture A

Happy and "up-beat" facial expression

Air under the arms, opening up the body language

Raised posture

"Beat-line" is higher and raises the eye-line of those watching

Balance is central (ie: equally balanced on both legs)

Picture B

You can see from Picture A that as well as looking uncomfortable and encouraging a bad back in later life, a "bad" posture is uninspiring to look at. As well as making you look less confident a bad posture will ultimately make the performers less inclined to look at you for cues, time keeping and inspiration during performance.

In Picture B you will note that the elevated posture and broadening of the upper body gives an air of confidence, helping to make you look relaxed and in control. An improved posture will hopefully mean fewer trips to the Osteopath too!

When the cast and band look at you - either down in the pit, or on a video monitor, they need to see someone who is in charge of the situation, and someone who is *leading* the performance. Your body should be centred (see exercise below), and there should be no extraneous movement (i.e. no un-necessary head, arm or body movements that will distract the players/singers or pull the focus away from your beat). It is also important that your body language is open and free. Set up a camera and video yourself practicing (also in performance if possible). Analyse your technique and take out anything you don't like. Always ask the question – "Could I follow that if I was in the band or on stage?" If you can't follow your own beat, how can you expect someone else to follow you?

Below is an exercise to help centre the body and encourage good posture.

- Lay down on the floor, place a book under your head and bend your knees upwards so your feet are flat on the floor Place your arms by your side, or gently resting on your stomach (*semi-supine*).
- Close your eyes and breathe slowly and deeply.
- Try to imagine that each part of your body is sinking in to the floor.
- After around 10 minutes roll over on to your side, and slowly get up.
- Stand tall with both feet firmly on the ground. Keep your feet slightly apart, and keep your knees soft.
- Imagine there is a piece of string at the base of your back, and that it runs up your spine to the ceiling. Imagine someone is gently pulling the string upwards. This will help to elongate your upper body and make you feel taller.

- Imagine you are holding two equally heavy bags (one in each hand), keeping your shoulders and arms loose and relaxed.
- Check yourself out in the mirror. Make sure your shoulders are at an even height (i.e. you aren't lopsided in any way). Often, if you carry a shoulder bag on the same shoulder each day you may find that this shoulder is higher than the other one, and that you may be holding tension in the carrying shoulder. Try to alleviate this tension by alternating which shoulder you carry your bag on. Ruck sacks (carried on both shoulders) are a good alternative to single shoulder bags as they spread the weight equally across both shoulders.

The Alexander Technique

Many performers use the techniques developed by F. Matthias Alexander to help with their posture. Take a look online at www.alexandertechnique.com for more information about the Alexander Technique. As well as displaying information specifically relevant to musicians the website also contains information about the usefulness of the Alexander Technique and an interview with the legendary British conductor Sir Colin Davis.

A CLEAR BEAT

The main purpose of the conductor in performance is to indicate and unify the beat so that the performers, both on stage and in the pit can play and sing as one body. It is therefore paramount that the conductor's beat is clear and easy to follow - otherwise there is no point in them being there!

Many conductors develop their technique over a long period of time. Some choose to use batons while other prefer to use their hands; some have a large flamboyant beat while others use a more economical technique. You should use whichever technique works best for you. There are several books that offer excellent guidance on conducting technique and I have listed the ones which I found the most helpful below:

- **Conducting Technique for Beginners and Professionals (Brock McElheran)**

- **The Art of Conducting (John Lumley and Nigel Springthorpe)**

- **The Modern Conductor (Elizabeth A.H. Green and Mark Gibson)**

Less experienced conductors should spend time studying the art of conducting before diving in to conduct a show (beat patterns, up-beats and various other *mechanics* of conducting technique are discussed in Appendix 1).

As with any other musical instrument it takes time to develop a solid technique that can be relied upon under the pressures of performance. This can only be achieved through hard work and practice.

REFLECTING THE FEEL OF THE MUSIC

The Musical Director is the driving force behind the music, and it is their job to enthuse the cast and band in performance through their dedicated and inspiring conducting. It is important that the beat reflects the "style" of the music. For example, you wouldn't conduct a slow lyrical 4 in the same way you would conduct a sharp military 4; likewise, you wouldn't conduct a slow, gentle passage of music in the same way as a heavy, moody passage. In simple terms, if you smile and look somewhat jolly whilst conducting a deep, dark emotional passage of music, you can't expect the band and cast to fully engage with your conducting. If you feel the emotions that flow from the music and lyrics, and can carry these emotions into your conducting, conveying them through your conducting style and body language, you will in turn find that the cast and band respond accordingly, as you all work towards a common goal.

- Film yourself conducting in various styles (conducting along to your favourite cast recordings is fine for this exercise) and see if your beat **and your body language** are reflecting the mood of the music. In practise, you will find that the band and cast will respond to this, and contrary to what some people say they do actually watch and take a great deal from the energy you give them.

- It is very easy to allow your energy to drop over time, especially during a lengthy run of a show. Work against this - there is no place for a passive conductor. Always inject your conducting with energy; this will in turn inspire an energized performance from your cast and band.

GIVING CUES

One of the Musical Director's responsibilities is to give cues to singers, instrumentalists and stage management. A cue may be an indication of when a performer needs to play or sing, or it may be a cue for the stage management to move scenery or initiate a new lighting state. When you are conducting you should also cue things that you like to hear such as subtle intricacies in the orchestration, or specific vocal nuances you enjoy - just as a good sound engineer will subtly lift things that they enjoy hearing in the mix. As well as encouraging the singers/players to enjoy performing their individual parts it also shows your awareness of the music, and your appreciation of everyone's individual contribution to the show. In the same way it is good to acknowledge when difficult passages are performed well - both on stage and in the orchestra pit. Musicians will often quietly stress over tricky passages of music, so it's nice to acknowledge when they play well. In the same way if something goes wrong, either on-stage or it the band pit the guilty party is often all too aware of their mistake, so a nasty glare from the conductor is generally not necessary. (It may on occasion be appropriate however, to give an acknowledgement of the mistake so that everyone knows that you are listening and fully aware of what is going on.)

- Always use **your eyes** when conducting. Your eyes are one of your main communicators and you should keep this in mind when conducting. Make eye contact with the musicians and singers - especially when cueing an entry. You need to ensure that your beat is at a height where those following can see both your beat and your face at the same time. If it is too low, it will be impossible to look at the beat and your face simultaneously; too high and it will be uncomfortable for you and cause excessive arm ache! Find a height that works best for you.

- It is common practice to conduct the beat with your right hand and cue with your left (regardless of whether you are right or left hand dominant in everyday life). The left hand can also be used to indicate dynamics and other performance indications. You should avoid mirroring the beat in your left hand as this is both distracting and a waste of energy. (Refer to Brock McElheran's comments in Chapter 8 of "Conducting Technique for Beginners and Professionals" for further thoughts on this.)

- Make sure that the way in which you give the cue reflects the cue you are giving. In other words, try to reflect the "sound" and feel of the cue as you give it. For example, if you are cueing a triangle "ping" (bright and crisp with a percussive attack) give a bright, crisp and "pingy" cue. If you are cueing a soft, placed string chord indicate the feel you want with a soft, placed and rounded (with no sharp "edges") cue. Rehearsal time is always precious, so the more you can express to the musicians through your conducting, the less time you will need to "explain" what you want to achieve, and more time can be spent actually playing the music (as opposed to talking about it).

GIVING CUES ON DIFFERENT BEATS

Practice cueing an entry on each beat of the bar. Imagine you are a wind or brass player playing the cue, and you need to breathe before you play. The cue should therefore feel like an up-beat (a breath) on the beat before the cue. Take care when you are practicing not to give your cue up-beat a "ping" as this can sometimes be mistaken as the cue point itself. The up-beat to your cue should start from a resting position on your beat line (with the feel of a preparatory breath) and then land on the cue-beat with a clear "ping". (Some conducting teachers liken the feel of the "ping" to touching a hot-plate with your finger tips.)

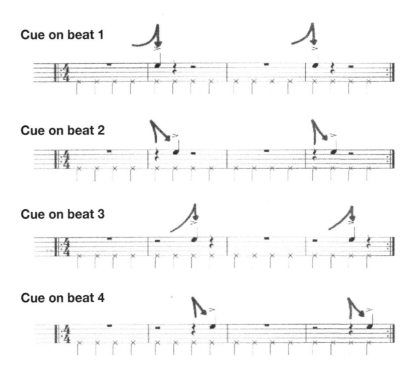

Cue on beat 1

Cue on beat 2

Cue on beat 3

Cue on beat 4

Exercise

Try practicing the above exercise using a small object such as a bean-bag or a small soft ball. Set your metronome to 100bpm and then practice scooping up your object on the beat before your cue, and then dropping it down so it lands exactly on the cue-beat.

GIVING A CUE ON AN OFF-BEAT

As a rule you should never beat an off-beat. If there is an accent or cue you want to give that falls on an off-beat you should give a punctuated cue on the beat before.

For example:

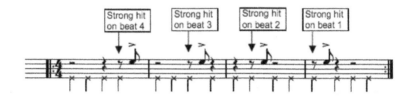

If you want to practice conducting accented off-beats one of the most famous examples to study is the opening of the first movement of Beethoven's 5th Symphony.

VAMPS

A *vamp*, sometimes referred to as a "Round & Round" (R&R), "Safety" or "Till ready" is a bar (or several bars) that you repeat until a spoken, sound or visual cue. Sometimes you "vamp" until a set cue, and then continue from the end of the bar (or the complete number of bars within the vamp) and other times you are instructed to exit (on cue) at any bar, half bar or sometimes on any beat. Vamps are often used at the start of numbers where the introduction music also serves as *Underscore* (more on this later).

Navigating Vamp bars can take some getting used to, and they can also be quite stressful to conduct due to their unpredictability. Here are a few thoughts on Vamps:

- If there is a cue line to exit the vamp encourage the actor delivering the line to say it the same way every time (i.e. the same speed and inflection). This will encourage a good type of routine. You will, of course, need to take extra care when working with understudies/covers as they will invariably deliver the cue line slightly differently.

- Let the actors know which lines of dialogue are cue lines so they can take care to deliver them clearly and consistently.

- When you are in a Vamp (vamping) take care not to give any movements that may indicate you want to leave the vamp ahead of when you do. In other words, keep the beat small when you are marking time, and then give a big, clear up-beat out of the Vamp when you want to continue.

- Make it clear to the band when you are waiting in a vamp. Many conductors find that making their beat smaller and indicating that they are waiting by simply holding their left hand in a "stop" or "hold" position is effective way to hold a vamp. When they want to exit they simply release the left hand hold position and give a big up-beat into the next bar (see photo below):

Holding a vamp
(Note that the left hand indicates the "hold" while the right hand marks time)

SAFETY IN NUMBERS

Sometimes if a piece of music has been rehearsed or performed over a period of time Vamp/Safety measures will start to become regular - so rather than being a "till ready" it will routinely be played 4 times (for example). In these cases it can be helpful for the actors and musicians if you indicate a count-down of the bars with your left hand (4-3-2-1) whilst marking time with your right hand (see below). That way the band and cast will know at a glance how may times round are left, and this will help eliminate anyone leaving the vamp a bar early or late. Never be afraid to state the obvious - even if you feel they are rock solid. If anything, it just makes it all that little bit safer!

ROUND AND ROUND AND ROUND AND ROUND AND...

When a Vamp appears in a score it is normally because something is happening on the stage that lasts an indeterminate length of time (either dialogue or movement). For example, there may be a vamp in the score with a note to move on after a certain *cue line*, or on a specific *visual cue* – such as when a specific character leaves the stage, or when a scene change has been successfully executed. Sometimes the cue to exit the vamp will be easy to anticipate (like a line of dialogue that you can easily refer to) whereas other times the exit cue will be more difficult to anticipate (such as when an object is thrown across the stage, or a cue that is based on an audience reaction). When you are conducting a vamp you have to think and act quickly in order to avoid delaying the continuation of the music.

KITCHEN PRACTICE

We can relate the different types of vamps to the following kitchen appliances:

The Vamp you can see approaching, and hence prepare yourself for (rather like an *Egg Timer* – by studying the amount of sand left in the timer you can make an accurate judgment as to when the timer will end).

The Vamp you know is close, but you can't pin point the exact moment the cue will arrive (rather like a *Kettle* – you can hear when it is close to boiling point, but it is difficult to predict the exact moment it will boil).

The Vamp you know is going to happen, but have no easy way of predicting the exact moment (rather like a *Toaster* – you know the bread is toasting, and you know this will take a matter of minutes, but with most household toasters there is little way of knowing the exact moment the toast will pop up).

Practise the following exercises, exiting the vamp as tightly to the cue as possible:

VAMP (1)

Cue: Put the kettle on

With a light bounce ($\downarrow$=116)   *Exit Cue:* As the kettle boils

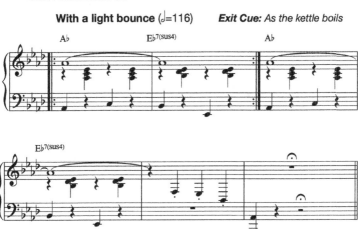

VAMP (2)

Cue: Start the egg timer

Exit Cue: Immediately after the egg timer finishes

[Exit after 2* or 4** bars]

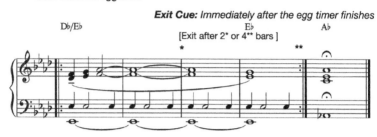

VAMP (3)

Cue: Put the toast into the toaster

Exit Cue: As the toast pops up!

[EXIT at any bar]

Customizing the exercise

Once you have mastered this exercise, why not try changing the cues to suit your personal surroundings. For example if you live near a road you could try vamping round until a car passes, or until a lorry or cyclist pass. If it's a busy road, maybe try vamping until 3 blue cars pass, or until a woman walks past. Alternatively, try popping the TV on and vamp until someone says the word "and". Make a list of different cues and practice jumbling them up so you never follow the same routine. This will help to keep you on your toes.

VAMPS IN PRACTICE

Below is a short extract from the West End musical "We Will Rock You" for you to practice on. In this number (Act 2: 2a "Flash") the Vamps are treated as bars of 1/4 so they can be exited on any beat. The idea is that you slightly pre-empt the end of the cue line to give a "3...4..." cue for the timpani and percussion crescendo into the sung entry: "Flash".

Start by listening to the recording of this number from the original London Cast recording of the show so you can get a feel for how it sounds. Once you are comfortable with the mechanics of conducting the number try to run it through several times with a friend saying the cues (ideally with different inflections each time) and if possible with a piano accompaniment.

Act 2: 2a - Flash

Words & Music by BRIAN MAY
Vocal Score by Mike Dixon & Brian May

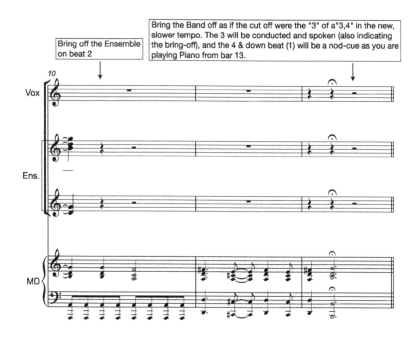

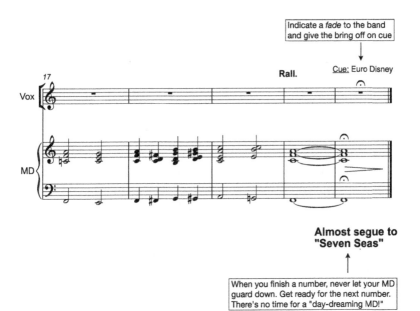

Indicate a *fade* to the band
and give the bring off on cue

Cue: Euro Disney

Rall.

**Almost segue to
"Seven Seas"**

When you finish a number, never let your MD
guard down. Get ready for the next number.
There's no time for a "day-dreaming MD!"

THE PIANIST/CONDUCTOR

You don't necessarily need lots of piano exam credits to your name to be a good show pianist or Pianist/Conductor. It is more about being a "functional" pianist who is solid and consistent. It is beneficial for all Musical Directors to be able to play the piano competently. Being able to play the piano will make it easier for you to learn the score as you will be able to work through it at the piano, studying the harmonies, vocal parts and orchestrations. You will also be able to play for the early work sessions with the writers (if you are working on a new show), as well as running songs with the principals and accompanying the ensemble vocal calls.

More and more Musicals nowadays are being conducted from the keyboard, so certainly in the professional setting piano skills are becoming more and more essential for the working Musical Director.

You should aim to develop your chord reading skills, as well as building up your dexterity around the keyboard. Try to pick up some riffs and "licks" in various styles. The odd "jazzy" run, or "poppy" riff can come in handy as part of your musical toolbox. If you are working on a pop/rock show may be handed a simple *lead sheet* (melody/top line with chords written above it) so on these occasions it is useful for you to be able to realize the chords into a piano accompaniment that will be helpful to the actors and dancers in the rehearsal room. Try to explore as many styles as possible at the piano. There are lots of well written Piano/Conductor (P/C) scores so try to get your hands on as many as you can, from *Oklahoma* to *Fame,* or *Beauty and the Beast* to *Rock of Ages.* Just by playing through them you will pick up some of the "feels" and "grooves" that, in time, will become second nature, and which you can keep with you as part of your piano vocabulary.

Piano/Conductor Score – P/C for short, also referred to as a Vocal Score. This normally takes the form of a piano reduction for rehearsal purposes (written to give a flavour of the orchestration), sometimes with important instrumental cues marked in (using smaller "cue" notes). The vocal lines are written above the piano part, traditionally with the lead vocal line is on a stave of its own (on the top stave), and the chorus parts written below, either on 2 lines (Soprano/Alto, Tenor/Bass) or on 4 separate staves (SATB-Soprano, Alto, Tenor, Bass). There are no hard and fast rules as to the form that P/C scores take. A well-written score will be clearly written with an accurate piano accompaniment; the vocal lines will be clearly marked indicating who sings what, and all the cue lines from the script will be marked in, along with guide metronome marks. A badly written score may be hand written, crumpled up and then re-photocopied several times with a skeleton piano part that bears little resemblance to the final orchestration, and vocal lines may be jumbled and the part divisions will need de-coding before the 1st rehearsal. In the case of Piano/Conductor shows (where the Musical Director conducts from the keyboard) there may be a separate Vocal Score (with a rehearsal piano part) and Conductors Score (written with the vocal lines, key orchestral cues and the Conductors performance keyboard part in place of the rehearsal piano part).

A SENSITIVE ACCOMPANIST

One of your roles as the Musical Director is to accompany the singers (either at the keyboard or by conducting the orchestra). It is desirable therefore for Pianist/Conductors to gain experience accompanying singers from the piano if the opportunity arises.

When accompanying:

- Focus on the singer's breathing. It is vital that you breathe as one (this is also true when you are accompanying/ conducting wind and brass instruments). The singer's in-breathe is effectively your up-beat so you should lock in to their breathing in order to marry your accompaniment with their vocals.
- Lock into the intricacies of the singer's individual phrasing and try to emulate this in your accompanying.

- Phrase the music as one - never let it become a battle between you both.

The Musical Director who is a sensitive accompanist will be highly thought of by the singers they work with. Accompanying is an art that requires careful practice. Being sensitive to a singer's wants and needs when you are accompanying at the piano will carry through into your conducting, and will in turn help to unify the singers and orchestra in the performances you conduct.

SIGHT-READING

Sight-reading is something many musicians fear the most! As the Musical Director you hopefully won't need to do a great deal of sight-reading, but you may find yourself playing for auditions and rehearsals for different productions during those times in-between jobs, and should therefore try to keep on top of your reading skills. You may be asked on occasion to play as part of a fellow Musical Director's band for a production, you may work as a vocal coach, play or deputise ("depping"/"subbing") on other shows as a keyboard player, or work as an audition pianist. These are all fantastic ways to practice your sight-reading skills, and also great ways to learn new repertoire.

I have found that vocal coaching is a great way to develop Piano/Musical Direction skills, as you get to play through lots of different repertoire with singers, and have the opportunity to explore the music together – studying and analysing the character and lyrics as you work through the song. You will go through a very similar process when you are working through the text with an actor in preparation for a production.

Picking up work as a piano accompanist for auditions is also a valuable use of your time. As an audition pianist you not only get to practice sight-reading but also get to see different Directors, Musical Directors and Choreographers at work. Less experienced readers will hopefully find it interesting to be in the audition room, and will learn a great deal by observing the process from behind the piano. More experienced readers may find it useful to see fellow Musical Directors at work, and may enjoy seeing the audition process from a different perspective, as well as practising their sight reading skills.

All these experiences will form a valuable part of your own personal musical melting pot, and you will be able to draw on such experiences in your working life as a Musical Director.

EAR TRAINING

Being able to play "by ear" is a useful skill for any musician to possess - in other words to be able to play without music or to extemporize around basic lead sheets or chord charts. As with all musical skills the more you practice, the better you will become.

* Spend some time working out familiar songs at the piano without the sheet music.
* Try to "busk" in as many different styles as possible. You can develop these skills by spending time playing through sheet music written in lots of different styles. Try your hand at classical, jazz, pop, rock, folk, etc. This way you can consciously and sub-consciously pick up some licks and phrases that are characteristic of each individual style.
* Pick a tune (any tune) and practice playing it in various styles. Make up versions of songs/melodies in "dreamy", "happy", "sad", "mysterious" and "romantic" styles. You will find that when you are working on a new musical you may sometimes be asked to do this with songs, so these skills are worth developing.

Another great way to explore improvisation is through playing along to "Silent Movies". If you are able to, spend some time listening to some old silent movie scores (whilst watching the film), and then have a go yourself at improvising along, to help develop a glossary of musical "clichés" (e.g.: chase music, scary music, romantic swells, dark underscore, mysterious music, haunted house music etc.) These will come in handy when you are working on devised theatre, Youth Theatre, Pantomimes, and in numerous other scenarios you may find yourself in.

Practise Improvising

You can pick up DVDs and Videos of some old Black and White movies quite cheaply ("Charlie Chaplin" and similar artists). Watch a few scenes, then mute the television and have a go at playing along yourself. This is a great way to develop your improvising skills.

WATCH.... AND LEARN

If the opportunity arises try to play as part of a pit band for a show. As well as gaining valuable experience playing as part of an ensemble and responding to musicians around you, you will see life from the other side of the podium, and will see how the band reacts to the Musical Director. You can learn a great deal by observing the Musical Director both as a conductor and as the leader of the band. Student Musical Directors should take the time to contact some professional Musical Directors and ask to sit in their band pits so you can watch them work. There are lots of different schools of thought on Musical Direction and it is good to witness first-hand as many of these different styles, methods and techniques as possible so you can develop your own individual style and make your own choices. (More experienced Musical Directors may also find this exercise worthwhile.)

A SOLID SENSE OF "TIME"

By it's very nature "conducting" is effectively *time keeping* for the band and cast. It is therefore imperative for the Musical Director to possess good "time". No one will ever expect a human metronome from you, but they will expect you to be able to set and hold a solid tempo. Below is a little exercise that I was taught at Music College* which really helped me to focus on my own sense of "time":

- Set your metronome to 50bpm
- Play crotchets (quarter notes) with both hands, taking care to ensure you land exactly on the beat. Really focus on the space/air in between the crotchets and make sure you are

as exact as you can be. It is often helpful to think of subdivisions (semi-quavers for example) in your mind so you have a way of dividing up the silence in between the beats.

- Play crotchets for at least 16 bars, and maybe longer (until you are confident that they are metronomic and evenly spaced, and that you are landing exactly on the beat)
- When you feel confident that your crotchets are "locked in" with the metronome, change the crotchets into quavers (eighth notes), taking care to ensure they are exactly half the length of the crotchets that you have just been playing.
- When you are confident that your quavers are locked in then go back to 4 bars of crotchets. Focus on the beats as well as the silences in between them. Ensure that you are landing exactly on the beat before moving on.
- When you are comfortable, move from crotchets to triplet quavers (triplet eighth notes). Again, play at least 16 bars of these ensuring they are even and secure before moving back to crotchets.
- Continue this exercise moving from crotchets to semi-quavers (sixteenth notes) and back to crotchets again when you are happy with your semi-quavers.
- Repeat this exercise going through the various note values.

The whole exercise is therefore as follows:
(Metronome: 50bpm)

1 (at least 16 bars) – 1/2 (quavers) – (1) -
1 – 1/3 (triplets) – (1) -
1 – 1/4 (semi quavers) – (1) –
1 – 1/5 (quintuplet semi quavers) – (1) -
1 – 1/6 (sextuplet semi quavers) – (1) -
1 – 1/7 (septuplet semi quavers) – (1) -
1 – 1/8 (demi-semi quavers) – (1)

* I am very grateful to David White for introducing me to this exercise.

Written out, this exercise looks like this:

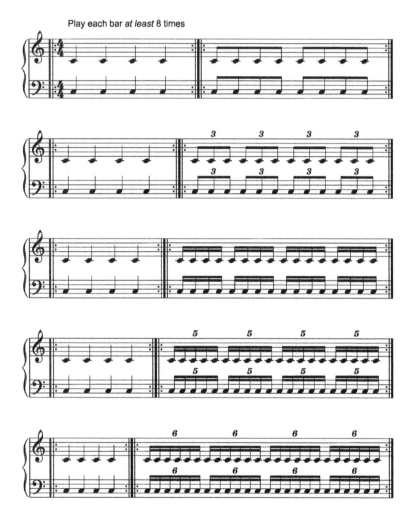

D.C.

You should practice this exercise regularly, and over time you will find your awareness for the beat heightened and your sense of time improved.

As a development of this exercise you can practice jumping between the sub-divisions. For example: 1 – 1/5 – 1/3 – 1 – 1/7 – 1/2 etc. *Be warned, this can become quite a brain-strain after a while!*

IT'S ALL ABOUT THE GROOVE

Being able to play with metronomic time is all well and good, but if the music has no "feel" it will probably sound dull and uninteresting. Pianist/Conductors must not only lead the "time" but also sit "in the groove". Many classically-trained musicians (especially pianists – whose practice time is mainly solitary) have not normally had the opportunity to play as part of a band or orchestra. Musicians with any kind of orchestral background will have experience playing as part of an ensemble, but a substantial amount of orchestral music has a certain fluidity inherent in the music, and therefore these musicians won't necessarily be used to playing "with a beat". Musicians whose background is based in bands (be it "Rock", "Funk", "Soul", "Jazz" etc...) have spent a substantial amount of time playing as a unit. You will often hear how a Bassist really "locked in with the kit", or how a Keys Player "sat in the groove."

As a Pianist/Conductor you will find yourself playing not only in the position that leads the show (i.e. the Conductor position) but also as a keys player who is part of the Rhythm Section. Both are equally important. A show that doesn't have solid musical direction will never be 100% solid – equally a band where one player in the core rhythm section doesn't sit in the groove, especially in a show like "The Wiz" or "Hair", is destined never to sound like it is really groovin'!

- Try to play as part of a band (any and every kind of band). Focus on *locking in* with the bass and drums. This is all about how it *feels* and how comfortable you are with each other's playing style.
- Listen to some pop, rock, funk, soul and jazz bands. Try playing along with any tunes that you like (chord charts for most jazz *standards* and pop tunes are available on-line), making sure you are locking in with the other players and sitting in the groove.
- If you are able to programme a drum & bass loop or get hold of a CD of some rhythm loops spend some time playing/comping/grooving along. It doesn't have to be flash or complex to be effective, so don't worry if the fancy licks are not flowing freely – it's all about feeling the beat, keeping a strong sense of time and rhythm – and most of all it's about locking in to the groove.

Observation

Next time you watch a live band keep a close eye on how they interact with each other. Note how the bassist and drummer lock into each other's groove, and how the musicians respond to each other's playing.

PREPARING TO CONDUCT FROM THE KEYBOARD

An increasing number of Musicals are now being conducted from the keyboard (i.e. you conduct the show whilst playing a keyboard part.) If you're lucky the keyboard part will have been written in such a way that you will be free to conduct the moments in the score that require it. However, there will be occasions when the keyboard part will be busier than ever at the exact moment you need both hands free to conduct. It is therefore important that you study and practice your Piano/Conductor score and work out exactly when and where you are playing, and when you are conducting (and with which hand). This should ideally be done **in advance** of the first band/orchestral rehearsal.

Although you would conventionally conduct the beat with the right hand there are many occasions when it will be easier to play with the right hand and conduct with the left. You should therefore aim to be an ambidextrous conductor.

Use the following exercises to practice playing and conducting at the same time:

"Hairspray", "Hair", "Mamma Mia", "The Wedding Singer", "Legally Blonde", "We Will Rock You", "Rock of Ages" and "The Rocky Horror Show" are all examples of mainstream shows that are conducted from the keyboard.

AMBIDEXTRAL BRAIN TEASERS

Conduct *in 4* with your Right Hand

Conduct *in 4* with your Left Hand

Conduct *in 3* with your Left Hand

Conduct *in 4* with your Right Hand

HEAD CUES

There will be times when you are conducting from the keyboard and need to cue an entry but both hands are tied up playing the part. At these times you may choose to give a "head" cue, or a cue "on-the-nod" as it sometimes called. When giving this kind of cue (as when you give a hand-conducted cue) it is important that the cue is given at the tempo of the music that you are playing (or in the case of a start cue, at the tempo of the proceeding passage of music.) This may sound obvious, but it is an all too common flaw of some conductors for the up-beat to be at a slightly different tempo to the proceeding passage of music, and for them to expect the musicians to auto-correct the tempo when they start to play. Take care to never fall into this category of conductor.

- Always breathe on the up beat of a head cue (as if it were the preparatory breath for a sung or played entry).
- Subdivide the up-beat in your mind as you give the head-cue. This will help to ensure that the cue is given in the tempo of the music, which in turn will make the cue clearer for the singers and instrumentalists who are following your conducting.

CUE LIGHTS AND COMMS

Cue lights normally take the form of a simple red/green lighting box, used for giving cues (often from the Stage Manager [SM] or Deputy Stage Manager [DSM] in *Prompt Corner*). Cue lights would normally be used at the start of each Act, and sometimes mid-show for cues which need to be timed to a specific stage/scenery movement. The standard cue light signals are: RED (standby) and GREEN (go). On the more advanced systems there will be a FLASHING RED (*are you ready to go?*). When you are ready you press the acknowledge button which will in turn make the flashing red turn to a SOLID RED (placing you on standby), and then this will be followed by the GREEN (go). Normally you will also be given a set of COMMS (either a headset with a microphone, or a one-touch telephone) so you can communicate with Stage Management (and sometimes the Sound Operator) before and during the performance. These are standard practises in both amateur and professional theatre.

This is an example of a telephone COMMS system. The phone has a button in the handle, so when you squeeze the handle the phone is activated. This particular system has 4 channels that connect to 4 different departments (including Stage Management and Sound).

An example of a cue light system:

On this particular system the **red** light is on the left and the **green** light is on the right. The acknowledge button is in the middle.

An example of a COMMS headset system. Rather than wearing the headset for the whole show it is common for the Musical Director to have it set up next to them so they can use it as required (normally before the start of each Act, or if there is a problem mid show.)

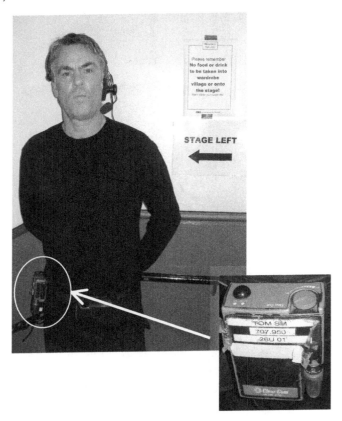

YOUR KEYBOARD/CONDUCTOR SET UP

If it falls to you to set up your Keyboard/Conductor position you should make sure that everything you need is easily accessible and you are comfortable with the set up. Below is an annotated Keyboard/MD (or Keyboard/Conductor) set up from the West End production of "We Will Rock You" to give you some ideas on how to set up your own position.

"WE WILL ROCK YOU" MD/KEYBOARD SET UP

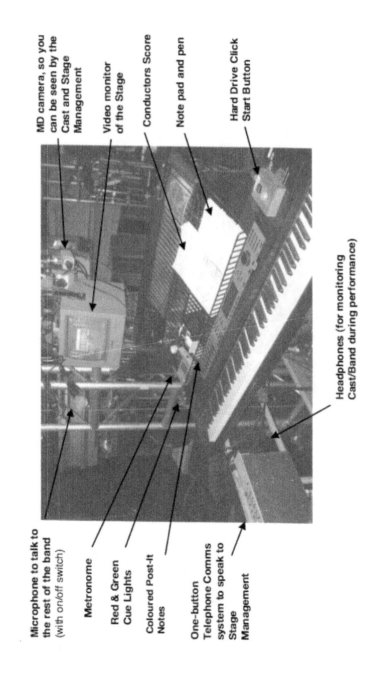

MD camera, so you can be seen by the Cast and Stage Management

Video monitor of the Stage

Conductors Score

Note pad and pen

Hard Drive Click Start Button

Headphones (for monitoring Cast/Band during performance)

Microphone to talk to the rest of the band (with on/off switch)

Metronome

Red & Green Cue Lights

Coloured Post-It Notes

One-button Telephone Comms system to speak to Stage Management

KNOWING YOUR WAY AROUND KEYBOARDS & SYNTHESIZERS

Whilst engaged as a Pianist/Conductor for an amateur/community or semi-professional show it is generally accepted that you will own or have access to your own keyboard - and that you will also know how to use it! On large-scale professional shows the keyboards will normally be supplied, but on smaller-scale/budget productions you may be required to provide your own.

As with all other technology, keyboards sometimes go wrong - so whether it's your own equipment, or it has been hired or bought for the show, it is useful for you to have a working knowledge of keyboard technology, since most shows nowadays (amateur, community and professional) use keyboards in some way or other.

Keyboards will normally be used to provide the piano sounds, and may also be used to either supplement the sound of the live instruments in the band and make it sound "bigger" (adding additional string, woodwind, brass and percussion sounds) through the use of synthesized sounds and samples; or they will be used to create sounds which are wholly synthesized; e.g. electric pianos, analogue synthesizer noises (square wave, saw waves), synth brass, choir and strings sounds, as well as warm pads and other "filler" sounds. A working knowledge of keyboards and synths will help you to:

- Problem solve when they go wrong.
- Programme sounds for your own shows/gigs.
- Understand what the score is asking for (i.e. when it says "soft Rhodes", "80's classic tines" or "B3 with Lesley on")

On larger/higher budget productions or when the keyboard part is more complex you may be fortunate enough to have a *Keyboard Programmer*. It will be your job (possibly alongside the Orchestrator if it is a new or newly re-orchestrated show) to liaise with the Keyboard Programmer and discuss which sounds you need.

Fender Rhodes – Classic 70s Electric Piano. They respond to touch so played softly they can be warm and smooth, and played harder the more "wirey" and dirty the sound gets. Commonly used in 70s funk and jazz. They are often enhanced with a "wah wah" effect. The intro to the Queen song "You're My Best Friend" is a good example of a Rhodes in action.

Tines EP (Electric Piano) – A more "belly" sounding Electric Piano sound. Used in almost every pop ballad in the 1980s! Have a listen to the Electric Piano used in the original recording of "I know him so well" (from "Chess") for an example of Tines EP.

Hammond B3 – The type of Hammond Organ most commonly used in Rock music. The B3 model *cranks up* particularly well to give a dirty, rock quality. Hammond Organs are often played through Lesley Speaker cabinets. The characteristic quality of a Lesley Cabinet is its controllable rotating speaker system. The Lesley control can be set to swirl slowly, or quickly (creating vibrato, tremolo and chorus effects). Many Hammond Organ models use a drawbar system to create different sounds, and the set up is similar to that of a Church Organ (using pipe lengths as reference point). Most good synthesizers will have some Hammond sounds already preset to the sounds you would expect to hear from an experienced organ player. Have a listen to "Whiter Shade of Pale" (mellow Hammond) and see if you can spot the cranked-up rock Hammond in the classic Rhythm and Blues tune "Gimme Some Lovin'"!

Roland, Yamaha, Korg and Kurzweil are the most commonly used synthesizer brands, although an increasing number of productions are opting to use computer-based systems as the source for keyboard and synth sounds. The most readily available software-based system is "Mainstage" which comes as part of the *Logic* sequencing and recording software. Basic programming skills (and often advanced programming skills) are a useful asset to any Musical Director, and can make you more employable – especially as so much in theatre now relies on this kind of technology.

Want to explore keyboards for free?

Most of the larger music shops have a selection of keyboards/synthesizers on display, so why not go in and have a play. This way, should browsing turn to buying, you will have a head start by knowing the makes and models you like. Technology advances quickly so if you want to stay on top of the game, check every 3-6 months for new stock.

THE SINGING MUSICAL DIRECTOR

Don't let the heading scare you off! This section definitely isn't about Musical Directors being amazing singers. It is however about Musical Directors not being afraid to use their voice in front of a group as and when the need arises.

All Musical Directors need to have an awareness of singing as they will spend a sizeable amount of the rehearsal process working directly with singers. If you are reading this as a School Music Teacher you are probably quite comfortable singing in front of a class. If, on the other hand, you have bravely volunteered to conduct the next show with a local Amateur Dramatic Society or Community Theatre group for the first time, then the thought of singing harmony lines to a room full of people may be slightly more daunting. As with the other muscles in the body, the muscles of the voice will strengthen the more you exercise them... so start singing today!

Scared about singing?

Why not contact a local singing teacher and ask if you can accompany their singing lessons for a day? Lots of singing teachers prefer to work with a pianist but can't always afford to hire someone. You can exchange a day of piano accompanying (and sight reading practice) for the chance to observe their teaching. Hopefully this will further your knowledge of the voice and you will also pick up some singing tips which you can put into practice at future rehearsals. Or why not add a note to the notice board at your nearest Music School offering to exchange piano or music theory lessons for some singing coaching? If you don't ask - you don't get!

WORKING WITH SINGERS

Familiarise yourself with some of the standard singing terminology so you can effectively communicate with the singers you are working with. Depending on the age and schooling of the performers you may find the same vocal style being described in several different ways.

One of the most popular singing techniques being taught in leading music and drama institutions is the *Estill Voice Technique* pioneered by Jo Estill. The terminology used in her teaching has become standard amongst singers working in all styles and genres.

Vocal Sounds (*Estill* terminology):

- **Belting** – A high-energy sound where the larynx is high and the vocal folds are thick. This sound is most commonly used without vibrato, and is often associated with the song's "money notes".
  🔊 Have a listen to the original cast recording of the last chorus of "Defying Gravity" (from "Wicked") as an example of female belting, or the opening of "Don't Stop Believing" (from "Rock of Ages") as an example of male belting.

- **Opera Quality** – A high-energy sound where the larynx is low and the vocal folds are thick. This sound quality is used in shows such as "Sweeney Todd", "Phantom of the Opera" and "Showboat".

- **Speech Quality** – This is the sound used in contemporary musical theatre in place of operatic recitative. As the title implies it uses the same vocal set up as everyday speech where the larynx is in a neutral position (not tilted) and is commonly used in the low range for women and the mid range for men. This sound is used in shows such as "Les Miserables" and "Miss Saigon" in the narrative-style sections (e.g.: the section where Eponine sings directly before "On My Own"). Speech quality is also widely used in pop music.

- **Mixing (singing with "tilt")** – tilting the thyroid cartilage (part of the larynx) as you move up the range will warm up the vocal tone and will also help to smooth out the "breaks" in the voice (the *passaggio*) thus creating an even tone across the vocal range.

  🎧 Have a listen to "Getting to know you" (from "The King and I") as an example of a mixed (tilted) female quality, and "On the Streets Where You Live" (from "My Fair Lady") as an example of a mixed (tilted) male quality.

- **Falsetto** – A vocal quality often associated with male singing, but that can be used by both men and women. Falsetto quality sounds intimate and reflective.

  🎧 Have a listen to the 1st verse of "God on High" (from "Les Miserables") as an example of male falsetto.

Other terminology you may come across for describing different vocal qualities:

- **Head Voice** – A term used for describing tilted sounds in the upper register. Head voice normally implies a lighter sound that uses more head than chest resonance.

- **Chest Voice** – A term associated with louder vocal qualities (normally without tilt). The singer will generally feel lots of chest resonance when singing in a "chest voice" – hence the terminology. "Chesting" a note in the upper register may be another way of describing a "belted" sound.

- **Bel Canto** – A term used in Opera meaning "beautiful singing". The term describes a seamless legato singing style employing a loose vibrato.

- **Legit. (Legitimate singing)** – A term used to describe "classical" singing qualities, often associated with mixed/tilted vocal qualities employing a more traditional vibrato. "Phantom of the Opera" and "The Light in the Piazza" are both examples of legit shows.

There are four distinct ways that a singer can start a note (referred to as the *vocal onset*).

- **Glottal Onset** – where the vocal folds are closed and they begin to vibrate at the point that the air passes through. This type of onset gives a clean and clear start to the note. ♉ Have a listen to the opening of "Good Morning Baltimore" from the original cast recording of "Hairspray". The first line: "uh uh oh" is an example of a glottal onset.

- **Aspirate Onset** – where the breath comes first, followed by the tone. Sing "h-ooo" as an example of an aspirate onset. This type of onset is sometimes used to give a seductive, "smoky" or tired feel. ♉ Have a listen to the first line of "The Oldest Profession" from the original cast recording of "The Life" as an example of an aspirate onset: "(h)-I'm worn out...."

- **Simultaneous Onset** – Also known as the "singers onset" or the "glide onset". This is where the breath and the tone begin at the same time. This onset is often used in classical singing styles. ♉ Have a listen to Jan Clayton singing the opening line of "If I loved you" on the original cast recording of "Carousel" as an example of a simultaneous onset.

- **Creek Onset** – This sound is normally associated with more contemporary singing styles whereby the vowel sound is preceded by a "creeky" sound. ♉ Have a listen to Michael Ball singing the first line of "Hushaby Mountain" from the original cast recording of "Chitty Chitty Bang Bang" as an example of a creek onset: "A gentle breeze..."

There are two distinct types of breathing:

- **The deep breath** - also known as inter-costal diaphragmatic breathing. This is were you breathe to the base of the lungs taking in a large quantity of air. This breath is normally quiet or silent.

- **The quick "surprise" breathe** – also known as clavicular breathing. This is a shallow breath taking air into the upper part of the lungs. This breath is often audible and can sometimes indicate surprise or excitement.

Twang is the sound created by tightening the aryepiglotic sphincter (AES), found in the upper part of the larynx. This tightening of the AES boosts the higher frequencies in the voice and has a brightening effect on the vocal tone. Twang is added to the voice by Musical Theatre, Pop/Rock and Opera singers (referred to as "squillo" in Opera) consciously or instinctively depending on the performer. It is used by actors, public speakers and singers as a tool to help the voice carry in large performance spaces and above the sound of a full orchestra. A "witches cackle" is an example of twang in it's purest form.

🎧 Have a listen to Sutton Foster singing the final section of "Astonishing" from "Little Women" as an excellent example of twang use. Listen to the bright qualities of the vowel sounds, especially in words like "astonish<u>ing</u>" and "<u>last</u>".

Vibrato is often added instinctively to warm and colour the voice and is a common feature of operatic, classical and M.T. (Musical Theatre) singing. If you are working on a rock/pop musical you may ask the singer to limit their use of vibrato or sometimes remove it altogether, since vibrato is used sparingly in pop/rock music. If you listen to Madonna, Bon Jovi or Lady Gaga for example you will hear little or no vibrato. That's not to say that vibrato is never used in pop/rock – Freddie Mercury, Adele and Meatloaf amongst others all use vibrato, but it isn't as much of a feature as it is in classical singing.

When coaching singers on duets (and sometimes in group/ensemble numbers) you may want to time the point that vibrato is used. This will help to unify the vocal sounds and will encourage the singers to focus on each other's voices. If you listen to the original cast recording of "As long as you're mine" from "Wicked" you will hear how the singers time the vibrato as one, holding off and adding at the same time to create a truly unified sound.

Try it yourself

As with many things in life, the best way to learn is with a "hands on" approach. Have a go at singing yourself, or even better – take some singing lessons. Explore the different styles of singing and learn how the voice works and how different sounds are made. As well as developing your own singing skills you should find that you are more able to relate to singers by having a clearer understanding of their craft.

VOCAL RANGES

There are several opinions on what the exact vocal ranges of each voice type are, so those listed below are intended only as a guide. In choral singing the common division is Soprano, Alto, Tenor, Bass - commonly abbreviated to SATB. Other voice types include Coloratura, Mezzo-Soprano, Contralto, Counter-Tenor and Baritone. In Musical Theatre the most widely-used four part division is Soprano, Alto, Tenor, Baritone, Each part can then be divided resulting in 1st Soprano, 2nd Soprano, 1st Alto, 2nd Alto etc.

The guide ranges for each part are as follows (middle C=C4), although it should be noted that many singers can successfully sing above and below these guidelines:

1st Soprano (Sop 1)	C4-C6
2nd Soprano (Sop 2)	C3-A4
1st Alto (Alt 1)	G2-E4
2nd Alto (Alt 2)	F2-E4
1st Tenors (Ten 1)	C2-C4
2nd Tenors (Ten 2)	C2-A4
1st Baritones (Bari 1)	G1-E3
2nd Baritones (Bari 2)	E1-E3

PUTTING ON AN ACCENT

There will be times when the actors are required to perform with a specific accent, different to their native accent (e.g. if you are producing a specifically *American* show in England, or vice-versa). If it is a professional production the management may decide to employ the services of a dialect/accent coach, however many smaller productions and amateur companies will not be able to do this and it will fall to the Director and Musical Director to ensure the cast are speaking and singing in the required accent.

For those who have never worked on accents before this can be quite a daunting task. In this case, it is worth investing in an Accent book* to help familiarize yourself with some of the basics (several books are accompanied by a CD containing useful examples and exercises). An *English RP (Received pronunciation)* or a *General American* accent are both good starting points, and you will find that there are several "rules" for each accent which you can make a note of and apply as appropriate. Once you have mastered the basics, you can attempt more regional British accents (such as Scottish, Welsh, Yorkshire and Cockney) and American accents (such as Brooklyn, Chicago, Southern American and New York.) *See the Appendix for some suggested further reading on Accents.*

A standard language used by singers and actors when working on accents is the *Phonetic Language* whereby each specific sound is given a symbol, thus making it possible to write a word exactly as it sounds. Phonetics is taught to singers and actors at many higher education institutions worldwide as an aid to learning pronunciation and accents. For those wishing to explore phonetics in depth please refer to the appendix for suggested further reading.

The best way to pick up accents is by listening to real people singing and talking in the accent you are working on. For example if you wish to learn a Wisconsin accent you should watch several TV episodes of "The Young and the Restless"; if you wish to learn a Yorkshire accent, watch several episodes of "Emmerdale" and really focus on the specific traits of the accent. Focus particularly on the vowel sounds and the speech inflections as these are the key to all accents.

AURAL SKILLS

The Musical Director should be constantly *listening* to what is going on around them. It is important that they should listen out for mistakes and know how to correct them. All Musical Directors should therefore aim to develop their aural skills.

TUNING

Keep an ear open for tuning/intonation problems in the band and cast during rehearsals and performance. A good musician will be able to hear if a note is very flat or very sharp, but if the intonation problem is more subtle then it may be harder to detect.

? Does the note feel too *bright*? If so, it may be slightly sharp.
? Does the note feel *dull*? If so, it may be slightly flat.

INTERVALS

The ability to distinguish different intervals can be useful in several ways. If you need to transcribe a piece of music, being able to recognize intervals quickly will come in very handy. Sometimes if a singer, or group of singers are struggling to hear or sing a specific interval you could try relating it to a famous tune that they are familiar with. This may prove to be helpful to them when they are practicing. Here are some examples of where different intervals can be heard in famous/familiar tunes:

Rising intervals:

- **Minor 2nd** – the first two notes of the theme from "Jaws"
- **Major 2nd** – the first two notes of "Strangers in the Night" ("Stan-gers in the...")
- **Minor 3rd** – the opening two notes of the English folk tune "Greensleeves"
- **Major 3rd** – the opening two notes of the Carol "While Shepherds watched their flocks by night"
- **Perfect 4th** – the opening two notes of "Auld Lang Syne" ("Should old....")

- **Augmented 4th** – the first two notes of the refrain of "Maria" from "West Side Story" ("Mari-a")
- **Perfect 5th** – the first two notes of "Twinkle Twinkle Little Star" ("Twinkle, twinkle...")
- **Augmented 5th/Minor 6th** – The first two notes of "Close Every Door To Me" ("Close Ev'ry ....)
- **Major 6th** – the first two notes of "My Bonny Lies Over the Ocean" ("My Bonnie...")
- **Minor 7th** – the first two notes of "Somewhere" from "West Side Story" ("There's a place.....")
- **Major 7th** – the first and third notes of "Bali Hai" from "South Pacific" ("Bali Hai")
- **Octave** – the first two notes of "Somewhere Over the Rainbow" from "The Wizard of Oz" ("Some-where over......")

Falling intervals:

- **Minor 2nd** - the first two notes of "I have a love" from "West Side Story" ("I have...")
- **Major 2nd** – the second and third notes of "When you wish upon a star" ("When you wish...")
- **Minor 3rd** – the first two notes of "Misty" ("Look at me...")
- **Major 3rd** – the 3rd and 4th notes of "Somewhere out there" ("Some-where out there...")
- **Perfect 4th** – the fourth and firth notes of the title line of "Master of the house" ("Master of the house...")
- **Augmented 4th** – the fourth and fifth notes of the title line of "Close every door to me" ("Close ev-'ry door to me....")
- **Perfect 5th** – the first two notes of the first line of "The way you look tonight" ("Some-day...")
- **Minor 6th** – the first two notes from the "Love story" theme
- **Major 6th** – the first two notes of "Music of the night" ("Night time....")
- **Minor 7th** – the first two notes of the refrain from "Something wonderful" ("He will not...")
- **Major 7th** – the second and third notes of the refrain of Cole Porter's "I love you" ("I love you....")
- **Octave** – the fourth and fifth notes of "The lonely goatherd" ("... a hill was a...")

Choir Practise

A great way to develop your aural skills is to sing as part of a choir/vocal group. As well as gaining an understanding of what it is like to sing harmonies as part of a group, it's also a great way to practice your singing. You'll also get chance to see vocal rehearsals from the other side of the conductor's podium and to see other Musical Directors in action.

THE ACTOR - MUSICAL DIRECTOR

Another part of the Musical Director's role is, working in conjunction with the Director, to marry the music with the character so that the songs can truthfully flow from the scenes in such a way that the dramatic line is continuous, hence making the character musically and dramatically unified.

In order to achieve this goal the Musical Director has to be dramatically aware – focusing on the acting as well as the music.

- Study the script so that you are familiar with the characters (more on this in Chapter 3)
- Listen to the inherent sound qualities of the actor's spoken voice and ensure that these qualities are also present in their singing voice (i.e. if their singing voice is considerably less resonant than their spoken voice, it may sound as if a different character is singing, even though it is the same person.)
- Consider the accents of the characters, and ensure that these accents are carried through into the singing voice (to a level that doesn't distort the singing).
- Always let the acting drive the singing - not the other way around. Even a pleasing voice can become tiresome to the audience if the acting does not engage them.

THE KNOWLEDGEABLE MUSICAL DIRECTOR

The Musical Director is actively involved in making artistic decisions that will affect the overall production, so it is important that these decisions are backed up with musical and theatrical knowledge. Just as the Director and Choreographer need to be aware of the set, costume design and lighting (as they relate directly to their own jobs), the Musical Director needs to be aware of anything relating to the music production and the overall sound of the show (such as Orchestration, the Sound department and Music Preparation.)

It is important that the people you are working with feel they can trust you, and this trust will be more easily attained if colleagues feel that you know what you are talking about, and you have taken time to study all aspects of your craft.

- Spend time watching and listening to as many live and recorded Musicals as you can. Whether you are at the start of your Musical Director journey or you are a seasoned professional, it is important to keep watching and learning. Musicals are being written, produced and re-worked all the time so never sit back and think "I know it all now" – you have to keep on learning in order to stay in the game. Never sit back and rest on your laurels!

A BACKGROUND KNOWLEDGE OF MUSICAL THEATRE

In order to make informed musical choices both in and out of the rehearsal room you need to learn as much as you can about the art form that is "Musical Theatre".

- Study the History of Musicals. There are some excellent books on the history of Musical Theatre and how it all began (see appendix for some suggestions). Learn about the journey from Opera to the early Musicals, and how the Gilbert & Sullivan Operettas led to the Broadway hits of the 1930s and 1940s. Study how the style of theatre writing has been influenced by world events, and how it has developed from the Classic Broadway Musical of the 1940s such as "Oklahoma" into more recent hits such as "Avenue Q" and "Wicked". Also, take time to compare Musicals from both sides of the Atlantic and note the similarities and differences between the Broadway style and the West End style.

- Study the key iconic, influential and famous Musicals. Listen to as many as you can, and spend time playing through the Vocal Scores at the piano.
- Listen to historic recordings, making notes on the style of playing and singing. Note the differences in the sound of the Orchestra and style of the singing between the 1930s/1940s and today. This will be helpful when making stylistic/artistic choices if you are conducting an authentic production of an older-style musical.
- The world of Musical Theatre is ever changing. Stay in touch with what is current, both in the West End and on Broadway. Use the internet to check out the various theatrical websites for information about new Musicals, taking time to read reviews and comments on new writing.

Web resources

Check out: www.whatsonstage.com, www.thestage.co.uk, www.broadwayworld.com and www.playbill.com

GET LISTENING!

It is impossible to write a "top 10" list of Musicals, but I think it worthwhile to list 10 brilliant Musicals which will give any newcomer a general and concise overview of Musical Theatre:

★ **Annie Get Your Gun**
  A classic, fun, traditional 1940s American Musical
★ **Guys & Dolls**
  Great songs! Nice story with good moral overtones
★ **My Fair Lady**
  A large-scale, strong, classic book-based musical.
★ **Sound of Music**
  A fine example of Rodgers & Hammerstein musical Genius!
★ **West Side Story**
  A superbly crafted Musical in every way!

★ **Cabaret**
Great songs, great story with dark undertones, superbly crafted by another legendary Musical Theatre partnership.

★ **A Chorus Line**
One of the longest running Musicals ever, for a very good reason! A meaningful true-to-life story with a great score.

★ **Cats**
One of a kind. A legendary piece of theatre, and a good example of Andrew Lloyd Webber's writing style.

★ **Les Miserables**
An iconic Musical Theatre masterpiece, finely crafted with a great story.

★ **Little Shop of Horrors**
A fun musical, written by a master tune-smith, and master lyricist, who brought the world many great Disney songs thereafter.

One for the shelf...

If there is just one Musical every Musical Director should own (CD, Score & DVD) it is undoubtedly "West Side Story". Sondheim's intelligent, moving, witty lyrics set to the rhythmic, romantic and emotional score by musical genius Leonard Bernstein is a master class in Musical Theatre writing. Based on "Romeo & Juliet", "West Side Story" should be studied by all Musical Directors, both as an exercise in how to craft a musical (lyrically and musically) and as a conducting exercise.

KNOWLEDGE OF ORCHESTRATION & INSTRUMENTS

There are times when it may fall to the Musical Director to amend, re-write, or devise orchestrations. If you are working on a smaller show (amateur or professional), having a working knowledge of orchestration can mean the difference between having a band and not having a band, as Producers are often reluctant to pay for a dedicated orchestrator and may sometimes expect the Musical Director to arrange and orchestrate the band parts (especially if you are working on a compilation or variety show.)

As most productions (Amateur, Community, Youth Theatre and Professional) work on a limited budget, you may be presented with a hired in set of parts written for 28 players when your budget allows only for a band of 8. At such times you may find yourself undertaking a sizeable amount of re-orchestration to make the music work for your particular production.

For these reasons I would recommend that all Musical Directors try their hand at Orchestration. The easiest way to learn is simply by getting stuck into it. Write some Orchestrations (or "Charts" as they are sometimes called) and get some willing friends to play them through for you to see what they sound like. Spend time studying tried-and-tested scores (ideally those which you are familiar with, and which you can easily obtain recordings of) as you will learn a great deal by studying how different textures and sound worlds are created, and how different instrumental techniques are employed to create different sounds and effects. There are some excellent books available on Orchestration. Please refer to the appendix for some suggestions.

If you want to delve deeper into Orchestration, spend time studying some of the key works of the Great Composers: (Beethoven: Symphonies, Tchaikovsky: Symphonies and Ballet Music, Rimsky Korsakov: "Sheherzade", Walton: Orchestral and Chamber Works, Elgar: Orchestral Works & Bartok's Concerto for Orchestra).

All Orchestrators should aim to have a thorough knowledge of the instruments they are writing for. The more familiar you are with the sounds a specific instrument can make, the more colours you will have in your musical palette.

- Take the time to chat to instrumentalists and ask them to show you around their instrument. Learn which tricks they can do, which range they sound best in, which mutes they can use and which different and unusual techniques can be adopted when playing them.

- An in-depth knowledge of the individual instruments will also be invaluable to you when you are conducting orchestral/band rehearsals. A working knowledge of the instruments will make you a more receptive conductor; you will have a clearer understanding of the technical demands of the instruments and the musicians will respect you for taking the time to study their individual crafts.

MUSIC WRITING SOFTWARE

There are several computer programmes that are specifically used to write musical scores. In particular, the two most popular are *Sibelius* and *Finale*. There are many benefits to inputting your scores into the computer:

- You can extract and print parts without employing a *Copyist* (see below).
- You can transpose, cut and edit parts without having to re-write all the parts and scores.
- You can use the playback function to listen to your orchestration using the computer's internal sounds, a soundcard or an external sound module. Whilst this gives a rather mechanical performance, sometimes with unrealistic sounds, it is a great way to check the score for misprints and voicing errors.

Copyist – the person responsible for preparing the Band/Orchestral Parts. Before computer software was readily available the Copyist would write out (by hand) the individual instrumental parts, copying them from the Score for each individual player. Now that many Scores are prepared directly onto a computer the Copyist's life is made easier, and their job has now become one of extracting and cleaning, rather than writing out by hand. The process of preparing and assembling the band parts is generally referred to as "Music Preparation".

A BASIC KNOWLEDGE OF SOUND

It is useful to have a basic knowledge of sound equipment and sound-related terminology. The Musical Director works closely with the sound team (which may consist of anything from 1-5+ people) on the overall shape and sound of the show. In smaller theatres and in schools and colleges there may be one member of Technical Staff who overseas the lighting and sound. In some provincial theatres there will be a Technical Manager and maybe two other staff – one responsible for sound and one for lighting. On larger professional productions the Sound Team will consist of a Sound Designer who designs what the show will sound like *front of house*, and who will decide what equipment is used, and one or several Sound Operator(s) who will mix the show on a nightly basis. Sound Operator Number 1 (often referred to as Sound number 1) will be in charge of the sound in the theatre/venue and they will be assisted by Sound number 2, 3, 4 (etc..) who will work backstage looking after the radio microphones and generally taking care of the sound equipment. They will also step in to mix the show when Sound number 1 is out of the building.

You should aim to understand the basics of sound set up and design, and the equipment that you come into contact with, especially in modern theatre where we see an increased use of keyboards, samples and computer systems. Here are a few terms you may come across and a brief description of each term:

DI Box	"Direct Inject" – where a sound source can be plugged into a desk, multi-core or sound-system without using a microphone.
XLR	Type of connector used to carry balanced audio signals.
Balanced	Wiring system that uses two out-of-phase conductors and a common screen to reduce the effect of interference.
Jack	(plug/lead) A commonly used mono/stereo audio connector.
Stereo	Two channel signal (left and right).
Back Line	On-stage instrument amplification.
Effects Unit	(FX) A device which adds an effect to the audio signal, such as reverb, delay, chorus etc...

Fader	A slider-control used on mixing desks and processors.
Foldback	A system used for sending mixes back to the performers (cast and band) so they can hear themselves independently from the **Front of House** (FOH) sound mix.
FOH	(Front of House) The sound in the main auditorium which the audience hears.
EQ	(Equalization) The ability to adjust the amount of high, middle and low frequencies of an audio signal.

Many musicians develop a fascination with all things technical – but be warned – it can become a very expensive and highly addictive interest!

Observation

You can learn a great deal about Sound by shadowing a Sound Operator during a performance. Sit with them out front at the desk and watch how they mix the show, noting how they blend the cast and band together to create the Front of House mix. This will give a greater understanding of the importance of the sound department and their role in the production.

CLICK TRACKS

Click Tracks are pre-recorded tracks containing a click (metronome) that the conductor/band can hear through headphones, and either vocal (and/or instrumental tracks) that are played simultaneously through the main Front of House PA system. Click tracks are being used more and more by amateurs and professionals in performance.

Click tracks (or "Clicks) may be used for the following reasons:

- To boost the sound of the on-stage vocals (especially useful for big "Dance" numbers where the cast find it hard to sing full out whilst dancing)

- To augment the sound of the band (using pre-recorded instrumental tracks alongside the real band).
- As a metronome for the band (where there are no other additional pre-recorded vocals/instrumental tracks - just a metronome "click" which the band can hear in headphones). These type of *Clicks* would be more common in "Dance" shows where the tempo has to be exactly the same from show to show for choreographic reasons, or where there are accurately timed set/scenery movements/video playback which are carefully timed to the music.

The *Click* is usually started by pressing a button – normally by the Musical Director but sometimes by the sound operator. The click track can be recorded on anything from a CD or Mini Disk (in the case of a simple 2-track recording – one being the click, the other being the additional track [vocal or instrumental]), or onto a more complex multi track hard drive recording system (capable of handling multiple vocal and/or instrumental tracks as well as the click).

Click Tracks are useful when you need to create a sound that is bigger than the vocal/instrumental forces at your disposal are capable of creating. They are often used for Cruise Ship shows and Holiday Park shows, as well as in more contemporary dance-heavy Musicals (as mentioned above). Be warned - Click Tracks can sometimes fail so it is best not to rely on them to such an extent that a performance could not continue without them.

Making your own click tracks

If you have access to recording equipment, you can prepare your own clicks by recording the "click" track onto the left channel of a stereo signal (standard left and right recording) and the vocal/instrumental tracks on the right channel (or vice-versa). When you play back the track in performance send the left output of your CD/Mini Disk/MP3 player to a headphone splitter/pre-amp (for the band to plug their headphones into so they can hear the click to play along with) and the right output to the sound desk to be fed into the Front of House PA system. If you prefer using a computer based system to fire the clicks, you can download *Q-Lab* which is software specifically designed for running sound effects and music cues in theatres. The basic version of Q lab is free to download from: figure53.com/qlab/

Chapter 3: **Preparation**

If asked for a basic description of what the *Musical Director* does, I would probably say "someone who *directs* the *music*". Quite literally that is what the Musical Director does – they *direct*. In order to do this effectively you must possess an in-depth understanding of what it is that you are directing, as others will look to you to lead and guide them on the journey to opening night and beyond. As the Musical Director, everyone will look to you for musical leadership and you will be seen as the pinnacle of musical knowledge for the production you are working on.

In order to fulfil these expectations you must ensure you fully **prepare** the Score so that you are in a position to answer any questions which the Cast, Creative Team and Orchestra/Band ask you.

READ THE SCRIPT

Before you start work on the score, and before your initial meetings with the Director, Choreographer and Designers, you should read the script *at least* three times. This will give you an insight into the characters and an awareness of the context of the songs within the story. Have a pencil to hand whilst reading, in case you wish to make any notes on the characters or on the musical cues/numbers. There will be decisions to make about the characters and about the ways which singers should approach the musical numbers. Knowing the context of the song and having discussed this with the Director and Choreographer before starting work is vital. The idea of a song flowing from the scene, the music being an integral part of the story and thus heightening the drama, is what Musical Theatre is all about, and it is your job as the Musical Director to help facilitate this.

Let's look at the powerful song "Maybe This Time" from "Cabaret" as an example.

If we didn't know the context of this song within the story there would be several plausible ways to interpret it. The "Maybe this time he'll stay" and the "...for the first time, love won't hurry away" could be taken from an "oh, woe is me...." viewpoint – i.e. my life is terrible, but *maybe* this time it might work. Or perhaps it could be read with a slight apathy - "*maybe* this time I'll be lucky...." *or maybe I won't*.

When we read the scene preceding the song we learn that Sally has just told her lover, Cliff, that she is pregnant. Because of her promiscuous lifestyle she can't be sure who the father is and so, just as she has done many times before, she will go to see the doctor and terminate the pregnancy. Cliff, however, wants to "turn over a new leaf", take a chance on the fact that he may well be the father and make a go of it with Sally. Before they have chance to finish their discussion the scene is interrupted by Ernst who has a job proposition for Cliff. With the prospect of supporting a mother and child Cliff immediately accepts Ernst's offer and they both exit, leaving Sally alone with her thoughts. Sally, now contemplating settling down with a steady boyfriend who wants to take care of her and provide for her, with the thoughts of motherhood entering her mind therefore sings "Maybe this time" with a sense of optimism - the half empty glass... *maybe this time*... is half full.

Armed with this background knowledge you would encourage the actress to carry this optimism into her singing voice - *sing it as you would say it* (a motto worth remembering). The sound should be light (with the larynx slightly raised) just as your speaking voice would be if you were speaking optimistically. The music begins softly so there is no need for the singer to over-sing the top of the number. Also note, Sally is alone on stage at this time and therefore has no need to raise her voice in any way. Any weightiness in the vocal tone could imply negativity, at odds with the mood of the scene preceding the song, and also with the lyrics themselves.

John Kander has set the lyric in the natural female "speaking" range so the singer should perform it with a "real" sound in a range that should never become too "singy" (and thereby detract from Fred Ebb's powerful lyric.) He has also left a great deal of space in the music which helps give the actor time to really *find* each line, and discover each new thought.

- If you look closely at the vocal melody line for the song you will see how it gently climbs upward as Sally's optimism grows. You can see that both the melody and accompaniment reflect the optimism shown through the lyrics in the lines "Maybe this time he'll stay" and "Love won't hurry away".

- Also note how the underlying accompaniment in the bass line of the whole number is this constant crotchet pulse - never changing, always there – perhaps a reflection of the fact that whatever happens: life goes on – something Sally is a great believer in.

This analytical process should be applied to the rest of the number, and to any other songs you work on. This gives you and the actor(s) plenty of "food for thought", and will, in turn, assist you in shaping the song so that it flows seamlessly from the scene, thus allowing the music to carry the drama forwards.

If you had you not read the script, thinking about the context of the song, and the journey the character makes as the song progresses (both musically and dramatically) you may not have interpreted it this way, and may have entered into an un-necessary discussion about how to approach the number – one which could ultimately have arrived at the wrong conclusion!

So…. the moral of the story is <u>always read the script!</u>

You should also research the background of the story, finding out about the composer, lyricist and book writer. Using "Cabaret" as an example, the musical was based on the play "I am a Camera" by John Van Druten, which in turn was inspired by Christopher Isherwood's novel "Goobye to Berlin" (part of "The Berlin Stories"). Although the lead character in "Cabaret" (Sally Bowles) is fictional she was inspired by Jean Ross, whom Isherwood met during his time in Berlin in 1931. The original musical was adapted into a film and new songs were introduced ("Maybe This Time" being one of the new songs written for the film version). Before directing the music for a production of "Cabaret" I would strongly recommend reading "I am a Camera" and "The Berlin Diaries", as well as watching the film versions of "I am a Camera" and "Cabaret".

If there are any shows which you enjoy listening to, but which you are unclear about the story, why not try to obtain the script/libretto and have a read*. As well as giving you an insight into the story behind the music, it will also be a useful exercise in script reading. You can then think about some of the issues discussed and try applying them to the music. The more you go through this process the more it will become second nature to you.

[*Samuel French on Fitzroy Street in London, or on 45 West 25th Street in New York has a great stock of scripts, also available on their respective websites.]

LEARNING THE SCORE

It is essential that you go into rehearsals with the score well prepared. When the time comes for you to rehearse the cast and orchestra it is important that they have absolute faith in your guidance, and confidence in your ability to conduct and lead them in performance.

The first stage of learning involves listening to the score in its entirety. This will give you an idea of the piece as a whole. Try to get hold of as many different recordings as you can and, wherever possible, use the original cast recording as your starting point, since this will often have been recorded under the supervision of the composer. If it is a new work, there probably won't be any recordings of the score (except maybe some demo tracks) so set aside several hours to play through the whole score at the piano and gain a feel for the writing style and overall shape of the piece.

Seek out any other study aids which may be available, such as recordings, films, archive footage, interviews, documentaries and books; and wherever possible go back to the roots of the work. For example, if you have been engaged for a production of "West Side Story", take time to watch the iconic 1961 film as well as listening to the 1985 recording which Leonard Bernstein made of the show. There is also a documentary about the making of this recording that gives an insight into both the work and the composer. Take time to watch this, as well as reading Sondheim's comments and notes on the lyrics (there are several comments in his book "Finishing the hat: The collected lyrics of Stephen Sondheim"). Seek out other recordings of the show and listen to how other Musical Directors have interpreted the score before you make your own musical choices. It is always worth looking on **youtube.com** for footage of various productions, interviews and documentaries that will give you a deeper insight into the background of the musical.

Once you have immersed yourself in as much information about the show as possible, you are now in a position to go back to the script and vocal score (where it all began) and start the score-learning process, studying each number in depth and making appropriate musical choices that will help to form the shape and style of your own production.

DE-CODING THE SCORE

You will normally be given a Piano/Conductor score to work from as opposed to a full orchestral score, both in rehearsals and often in performance as well. The Piano/Conductor score (or *P/C*) will often contain lots of information and cues that are helpful when it comes to conducting, but not so helpful when crammed in as part of an already busy Piano accompaniment. You should therefore take time to de-code the score *before* you enter the rehearsal room for the first time. Reduce the score so that it gives the singers the cues that they will hear when the band joins, also making sure you are comfortable playing the score in the rehearsal room (assuming you don't have an able-fingered rehearsal pianist working with you). You can take out some of the fast string runs and woodwind flourishes that colour the orchestration (normally cued in little notes in the P/C score) instead bringing out the chords and harmony that gives the singers their notes and cues. You may also need to keep time - even by just playing bass notes during drum/percussion/dance breaks so the music doesn't stop, allowing the dancers and singers to hear where the beat is.

GETTING YOUR HEAD OUT OF THE SCORE

You should try to get the score under your fingers and into your brain as early as possible. It is better to use the score as a reminder and safety net (both in rehearsals and in performance) as opposed to actually reading it all the time. When the actors and musicians look to you for guidance it is important that they see someone who is aware of what they are singing and playing and is with them 100%. It is rather uninspiring for them when looking to you for guidance, to see your head buried in the score. You should endeavour to be musically omni-present, which will make everyone around you feel confident, safe and secure.

Next time you go to see a Musical try to watch the Musical Director in action. Observe how much eye contact they make with the actors and musicians, and how little they actually read the score whilst conducting.

PREPARING TO TEACH THE SCORE TO THE CAST

When you are learning the score you should mark onto it all the musical nuances that you plan to teach. This will save you time in the rehearsal room as there will be less musical choices to make in front of the cast. I usually teach the musical intricacies in the same rehearsal that I teach the notes, which ensures that the cast learn the finer details at an early stage, and they are more likely to retain this information through the rehearsal process and into the performances. (Normally I rehearse each individual harmony line several times, then run the sequence with all parts together several times; then I add the nuances in the same rehearsal so the cast leave with all the musical information they need.)*

You can use your discretion regarding what to do "on the shop floor" (i.e. as you go along) and what is better to have planned in advance. Some of the things you should consider are:

- *Diction & Pronunciation* – Clear diction is of paramount importance in any musical. Most would agree that the vowel carries the tone whilst the consonant carries the meaning. You should therefore encourage good diction from the company at all times. If the audience can't understand the lyrics, how can you expect them to fully engage with the story?

  Whilst studying the lyrics you should begin by reciting them out loud. Make notes of how you *naturally* say each sentence. Do any consonants feel weak or difficult? If so, then you will need to highlight these as areas for the cast to focus on, otherwise the may be lost in performance.

*Some other Musical Directors prefer to layer on the musical nuances at a later date, and whilst I respect their different working practises I have always found that the method described above has achieved the best results for me.

Are any words tricky to say, and does it feel unnatural to pronounce certain consonants at the end or start of words when you recite a whole sentence?

For example, if you recite (at show tempo) the title line of the song "At the end of the day" from "Les Miserables" (without any pre-meditated analysis) do you find that what you are actually saying is: "A(t) the end of the day"? To most people it would feel unnatural to pronounce the "t" of "at" and if you were to insist on a company doing this in performance the result would probably be rather messy. "A(t) the end of the day" is certainly how you will hear it in nearly all recordings of the song (including the original London and Broadway cast recordings). This is an example of where it is right to drop a consonant so the lyric feels and sounds natural to the listener.

Another example of this is in the chorus from the "Guys and Dolls" number – "Sit Down, you're rocking the boat". Begin by reciting it up to show tempo exactly as it is written:

"For the people all said sit down, sit down you're rocking the boat"

If you insist on a cast highlighting every single point above you will find yourself with a tired, frustrated and tongue-tied company (and you'll probably find no one wants to sit with you in the coffee break!). A common way to tackle this line, which probably feels more natural would be as follows:

"Fo the peopl..all sai(d) siddown, siddown yarockin' the boa(t)"

This is how most people would say the line (at speed) and certainly the way you will hear it on most, if not all, commercial recordings. *Sing it as you say it* is a motto worth remembering when planning and rehearsing diction. Strive for clarity but take care not to push to the point where the lyrics are over-pronounced, as this will only make the music sound pedantic and unnatural.

You should also spend time thinking about accents. What accent is being adopted for the show, and what implications will this have on the singing/pronunciation? If the dialogue is in General American then the actors should obviously sing in General American.

There may be times when either you or the performer will choose to modify the vowel sounds so the song is easier to sing. This is common practice when a singer has a particularly exposed high note. For example, on a word like "you" if a singer opens up the vowel slightly by lowering their jaw whilst singing, the resulting sound may be more open and be easier to sing. However, if the singer opens the vowel sound too far (so it is more like an "Ah" shape) the resultant sound will be more like "yAW" than "you". It may be easier to sing but it sounds like a different word! These vowel distortions are taught in several leading institutions, and, if done well, can be extremely effective. However, many singers have a tendency to take them too far so be vigilant, otherwise a phrase like "We will, we will rock you" can easily become "We wELL, we wELL, rAHck YeAAAAAHoo"!

♀ To hear an example of how vowels can be modified to serve both the performer and the song effectively listen to the original cast recording of Sutton Foster singing "Astonishing" from "Little Women". In the penultimate phrase you can hear how she modifies the vowels in each of the three different "Astonishings" to create the best sound, without distorting the word. If you listen carefully you will hear her sing: "astonish-*eee*-ng, aston-*eh*-shing, astonish-*eh*-ng"

• *Try it out* – There will be times when you wish to try several options for the pronunciation of a specific line with the company to see which way is the most effective. Don't be afraid to do this. There are often several "correct" ways to do something, and as the Musical Director you have the right to try things out before making a decision on which works best for you and your company. As long as you have tried it for yourself to make sure you are not asking the impossible, it's always fine to try things out in the rehearsal room.

- *Breathing* – If the musical phrases marry the natural lyric phrases, the breath points will be obvious and won't need clarification from the Musical Director. Sometimes the phrasing won't be quite so obvious and a decision about where to breathe will need to be made. If you are working with a soloist you can decide the breath points together, but if you are working with an ensemble you will need to tell the group as a whole where to take a breath as breathing in different places can sound ugly and may break up the flow of the lyrics, distorting the meaning of the line. As a rule you should avoid putting a breath point in the middle of a line (or worse still, in the middle of a word) for the simple reason that you wouldn't usually do this in everyday speech and the phrase will sound unnatural when sung. Many performers will instinctively take a breath before the final chord, especially in a full-on Company number.

If you look at the example below, taken from "Merrie England" by Edward German, you can see that taking a breath before the final chord not only breaks up the line, but also breaks up the final word. In this instance you would therefore rehearse taking a breath before the final "Merrie England" (marked with a tick* in the written out example below) or even taking the whole last phrase in one big breath (marked with a bold tick). This is something you could try out with the cast in the rehearsal room. If the final chord sounds weak or the cast are short of breath, you could ask the Company to take a big breath before the final line and then snatch another "top-up" breath before the final "Merrie England". It is worth noting that if there is an impractical melodic line where a breath is absolutely necessary, but you don't want the musical line to be broken by a Company breath, you could try *staggered* *breathing*, where the different members of the company breathe at different times. Assuming the ensemble is large enough, this will create the illusion of a continuous line with no obvious audible breath to the listeners. If you are planning to use staggered breathing it may be helpful to set specific breath points with the company to avoid everyone gradually drifting back to the same breath point.

Note that a tick is the standard breath mark, but you may choose to develop your own shorthand.

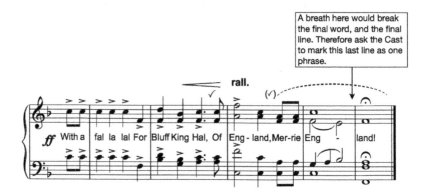

A breath here would break the final word, and the final line. Therefore ask the Cast to mark this last line as one phrase.

Further study

Another example is "You'll never walk alone" from "Carousel". The final reprise is sung by the full company with the closing cadence landing on the "lone" of "alone". Some singers may instinctively take a breath before the final chord, and thus break up the word. On this occasion, you would tell the company to mark in a breath before the final word, and phrase over the final choral cadence. Also, if you ask the company to put a strong "K" on the word "Wal_k_" firmly on beat 4 (before they breathe), this will ensure a clean, clear ending to your performance. The practice of breathing off a consonant is a useful technique to ensure the Company breathe as one.

- *Think about the meaning of the lyrics* – When studying the lyrics you will invariably be asking yourself what meaning they are trying to convey, and why the characters are singing them. When working with principal actors, decisions about character and meaning will normally be made in rehearsals with the actor, the Director and the Musical Director (sometimes with input from the Choreographer). When working with an ensemble on the interpretation of the sung lyrics it often falls to the Musical Director to make these choices, so it is helpful to plan in advance which are the "key words"; in other words, which words do we need to hear to understand the meaning of the lyric? If we lift these words when we sing the line, it can help the audience (sub-consciously) to understand the meaning of the text.

When working on the lyrics you should keep in mind that any word that falls on a strong musical beat (i.e. a word that lands on beat 1 of the bar, and beat 3 in 4 / 4 etc...) already has a built-in musical stress. Good writers will have helped by placing important words on strong beats. If there is an interesting or important word that falls on a weaker beat, and you ask the cast to highlight/bring out that specific word, you will hopefully find this helps to lift the lyrics off the page.

Let's use an example from the chorus of "Merano" from "Chess":

"<u>Oh,</u> I get high as I <u>saunter</u> by the <u>mou</u>ntains of Mer<u>a</u>no. Hum<u>ble</u>, shy Mer<u>a</u>no, <u>flouri</u>shing to a <u>fault</u>."

Sir Tim Rice has done most of the work for us, since many of the key words that give this lyric it's meaning and excitement already fall on the strong beats (<u>underlined</u>). If you highlight some of the interesting words that *don't* fall on the 1st beat of the bar you can give an added lift to the text, as the ear will be drawn to the less obvious musical stresses, making the text truly sparkle (which is right for this song in the context of the show):

"<u>Oh,</u> I get **high** as I <u>saunter</u> by the <u>mou</u>ntains of **Mer**<u>a</u>no. Hum<u>ble</u>, **shy Mer**<u>a</u>no, <u>flourishing</u> to a <u>fault</u>."

If we lift the words in **bold** type, we will find that, if combined with the natural musical stresses already written (underlined), it really works a treat! This may seem like a small thing to do, but when working with a chorus on numbers like this you need to work much harder, as the multiple voices (especially those singing in unison – as above) can often make the music sound heavy and the lyrics may get lost in the sound.

It is also fun when working on music that is quite "wordy" and fast flowing to experiment with different types of phrasing. For example:

"Oh I feel great in this bouncing state, Oh hail to thee Merano"

You can experiment with this, making the first half of the line "bouncy", thus further accentuating the lyric, and the second half of the line more *legato*, using longer vowel sounds and making the effort to stretch out the words. This should make it feel more regal and reverent – "Oh hail to thee Merano". Changes in the phrasing will help to lift the lyrics off the page, and help to keep the audience's attention. Wordy passages can very easily sound monotonous, especially when sung by an ensemble, so any device that can be used to break that monotony is worth trying.

The more voices there are, the harder they will have to work to achieve an energized and exciting sound, and the more accurate and precise their execution will need to be in order to make it work.

MAKING ARTISTIC CHOICES

As well as the "technical" choices discussed in the previous section, there will be artistic choices for the Musical Director to make about the interpretation of the lyrics (in consultation with the Director and the rest of the artistic team.) These decisions should be based on your knowledge of the piece and of the characters, your knowledge of the appropriate musical style, your knowledge of which techniques work in practice and finally your personal musical taste.

Here's another working example for you to think about:

- Looking at the lyrics from the finale of "Tommy", you can see there are some choices to make about pronunciation and interpretation:

    "Listening to <u>you</u>, I get the <u>music</u>,
    Gazing at <u>you</u>, I get the <u>heat</u>.
    Following <u>you</u>, I climb the <u>mountain</u>,
    I get ex<u>citement</u> at your feet."

    As in the previous example the strong musical beats/stresses are underlined.

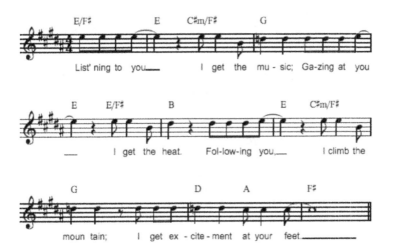

The choices we need to make are:

1. What meaning do we wish to convey?
2. Are there any diction points that may sound messy if we don't clarify them?
3. Do we need to plan the breathing, or is it intuitive?
4. Are there any accent issues?

Let's address each point in turn:

1. When looking at the meaning, you need to take the lyric in the context of the storyline, considering the character(s) and their journey so far. Choices will need to be made regarding where the stresses are and what "points" you feel need to be conveyed through the lyric. As the Musical Director your job is always to help facilitate the *acting through song*.

These are the choices that I made (after discussions with the Director) and they worked well for me. You may find a different solution which works equally effectively for you and your Company, and such variety is what keeps this profession fresh, allowing all Musical Directors to put his or her individual stamp on a show.

(This song comes at the end of the show, and is often interpreted as showing reconciliation between Tommy and his family).

Listening to you, I get the music – *When I listen to what you are saying, I understand the music, and all that surrounds the music*. Hence the stress lands on GET. If we make the music the stress we are simply adding weight to a word that falls on a strong musical beat and therefore already has a musical stress. This is less interesting than stressing the GET (meaning "understand" in this case). In the story, situations arise where people don't take the time to learn about and understand each other, which is why I feel it is right in the finale (written with a powerful, choral, uplifting musical feel) to show through the lyric that they are now just beginning to understand one another.

Gazing at you, I get the heat – *Literally "when I look at you, I feel warm – and you give me warmth".* It is important to the characters that they are gazing at <u>you</u> as it is <u>you</u> that is now giving off warmth – as opposed to anyone else. On the same note it is <u>warmth</u> that you are giving through the feeling of reconciliation, and it is important that we feel the <u>heat</u>. When studying lyrics I often ask the question "what word(s) would we alter to give the opposite meaning?", and the answer tells me which word is most important in that sentence. In this case the opposite for me would be: "gazing at someone else, I feel cold". The stresses therefore become: "Gazing at <u>you</u>, I get the <u>heat</u>". Also note that these stresses fall in different musical places to the previous line. This, in itself, is a useful musical device to use.

Following you, I climb the mountain – This is perhaps more difficult to analyse. We could interpret that if I <u>follow</u> you (either literally or meaning "follow your guidance") I climb the mountain (a metaphor meaning to rise to a challenge, or to <u>work</u> at something, i.e. a relationship.) We already know that there is much rebuilding of relationships to be done at the end of "Tommy". Hence we could say "<u>Following</u> you, I <u>climb</u> the mountain" (<u>with</u> you I can <u>rise</u> to the challenge).

I get excitement at your feet – *I get <u>excited</u> when I am at your feet.* "At your feet" could be a way of describing when I look up to you, or being "at your feet" in a reverent way, namely laying down at your feet. This line is therefore about the <u>person</u> and not about the feet. I get <u>excited</u> when I am at <u>your</u> feet - "I get <u>excitement</u> at <u>your</u> feet".

I picked this example since it is a tricky one to work on. I have not found a definitive meaning of this chorus, and those who are familiar with the show (or the film) will know that "Tommy" is not a clear-cut storyline, and can be interpreted in several quite different ways. For this reason I have shown you my own analytical process, in the hope that it will encourage you to really think about the lyrics and ultimately arrive at your own conclusions.

2. When thinking about the diction we must proceed with caution with this particular example. It is important in **any** rock/pop show that the singing sounds *real* and not *theatrically affected*. By it's very nature choral singing (as this number essentially is) can sound very *un*real – because if you think about it, people don't spontaneously burst into harmonious singing in real life situations. On the flip side, if the diction isn't clarified the words may become messy and unclear, and the audience won't be able to understand what's being said. This is another example of "sing it as you would say it". When I say it out loud, this is what feels natural to me:

"Listenin to_you, I ge_the music, gazing_at_you, I ge_the heat.
Following_you, I climb the mountain, I ged exci(d)men_tat_your **feet**."

For me, this feels like a natural way to say the lyrics. You may find a different way around it.

3. The only breathing issue which may arise would be if anyone tries to snatch a breath mid-way through a line, in which case you'd simply ask them not to. In this example there is no reason why you can't sustain the melodic line by taking a breath at the end of each phrase. As this is not traditionally a "dance" number the cast should not find themselves out of breath mid-line. In heavily dance orientated shows such as "Fame", "Saturday Night Fever", "Chorus Line" and "42nd Street" where the performers are required to dance and sing at the same time, you will often find they need to snatch a lot more breaths, often mid-phrase and sometimes mid-word. Although this is a musical compromise you sometimes have to concede to what is practical; If you have ever tried to dance and sing at the same time you will fully understand the difficulties!

4. The only accent issue that may arise with this example is that "Tommy" is very much an English musical and therefore you should keep an ear open for any

American inflections that may creep in (as they often do in Musical Theatre singing on both sides of the Atlantic.)

If we put everything we have discussed together we arrive at this:

"Listenin to_you, [v] I ge_the music, ✓
Gazing at_you, [v]I ge_the heat. ✓
Following you, [v] I climb the mountain, ✓
I ge(d)exci(d)emen tat_your fee____t." ("t" – off on beat 6)

(note: there is no optional breath in this last line as it would break the sentence)

KNOWING THE LYRICS

As you are studying the lyrics in preparation for rehearsals and performance you should endeavour to commit them to memory wherever possible. This way you can mentally sing along with the show, and if someone *dries* on-stage, you can mouth the words and help them out. Knowing the lyrics inside out will also help you to fully enter into the music and the story, which will in turn help you to shape the music around the lyrics and reflect the dramatic story in your conducting. If your body language and expression reflects the mood and feel of the music, you should find the actors and musicians respond to this, which in turn enhances the overall performance.

Drying/Dries – When an actor "dries" on-stage, it means they forget their lines, or lose their train of thought. In amateur theatre there will sometimes be a "prompt" (often the Stage Manager [SM] or Deputy Stage Manager [DSM]) who will read the line to the actor from the wings (the areas just off-stage on either side, masked from the audience) so they can continue. For professional productions the actors are normally left to find their own way through without the aid of a prompt (but often with the help of their fellow actors). In a Musical, if a performer dries during a song they will often look to the Conductor in the pit for help, so it's great if you are familiar enough with the lyrics to be in a position to help them out.

CUE LINES AND WARNING LINES

The *cue line* is the line of dialogue that directly precedes a musical number. It is important that you familiarise yourself with these lines of dialogue and mark them clearly in your score.

When preparing your score for rehearsals and performance it is worth marking in the cue lines as early in the process as possible (assuming it isn't a new work where the script is being revised on a daily basis.) This way they will start to ingrain themselves in your memory and cueing the songs directly from the preceding dialogue will become second nature. Keep the script close at hand in rehearsals so that you can note any cuts and changes that are made. You should also mark the *warning lines* in your performance score. *Warning lines* are for your reference only, and act as a preliminary cue giving you time to get ready for action. It is important that both you and the musicians are ready to play the moment you hear the cue, so the warning line serves as your cue to get ready for the main musical cue.

Be very specific in the way you mark your cue lines. There are times when you will need to cue a musical cue/number on an exact word, so rather than underlining an entire cue line you should be specific and underline the exact cue word in the cue line.

Look at the following example taken from the "We Will Rock You" script written by Ben Elton:

> KHASHOGGI: Put them together and what do you get?
> KILLER QUEEN: Alchemy Khashoggi, pure Alchemy
>
> *Song 8 – "It's a Kind of Magic"*

If you were to underline the whole cue line how do you know exactly when to give the up-beat? At the start, middle or end of the line? If you underline the exact word you can be very precise about exactly where the music begins.

> KHASHOGGI: Put them together and what do you get?
> KILLER QUEEN: <u>Alchemy</u> Khashoggi, pure Alchemy
>
> *Song 8 – "It's a Kind of Magic"*

Note that "It's a Kind of Magic" begins with a sound effect that starts from nothing and builds over a few seconds. It is therefore necessary to cue the music at the start of the cue line as opposed to the end, in order for the effect to reach full volume when the dialogue finishes.

CONDUCTING PASSAGES OF UNDERSCORE

Underscore (U/S) also referred to as Under Dialogue (U/D) refers to a passage of music that is played underneath spoken dialogue, or to accompany all or part of a scene. Sometimes passages of Underscore music can be relatively short (only several bars long) and on other occasions they can be quite lengthy, spanning several pages of music.

Some Musicals have sections of Underscore that serve as a long introduction to a song, allowing the musical number to flow directly from the scene (such as the "Balcony Scene" from "West Side Story"). There are also numerous examples where sections of Underscore are contained within the middle of a song (such as Act 1:number 5 from "Carousel": the sequence incorporating "If I loved you" or "Night Waltz" from "A Little Night Music") and even those which are musical numbers (or musical "cues") in their own right (such as music cue 24f from "City of Angels": "The Tennis Song – Underscore").

When conducting (or playing) Underscore that needs to fit under a section of dialogue, it is helpful to give yourself "markers" or ghost cues so that you can monitor where you are in the dialogue. Often with Underscore, the start and end points (or approximate end point) are defined in the script, but there are no specific cues that have to match in the middle. In some cases there may be one cue in the music that is intended to match a specific line of dialogue, but the surrounding music is free and not directly related to specific text. Unlike working to cue lines, Underscore tends to be freer, and since sections of dialogue can be quite long and will often involve more than one speaking character, they can vary considerably in length from show to show, especially when understudies are performing.

PRACTICE MAKES PERFECT

The following example is a passage of Underscore written to accompany the famous World War 1 poem "In Flanders Fields" by Major John McCrae. You can see that guide dialogue lines from the poem have been written in this example, so you can keep track of where you are in the music. It is then possible for you to *stretch* the music, or "push and pull" the tempo (ideally so it is imperceptible to the listener), so that the music lasts for the length of the poem.

Musically, the breakdown is as follows: 1st paragraph = bars 1-4, 2nd paragraph = bars 5-8, 3rd paragraph = bars 9-14. Taking this breakdown as guideline cues (marked into the score), you can push and pull the music accordingly (*rubato*) to make it fit with the poem.

In Flanders Fields
By Major John McCrae, May 1915

In Flanders fields the poppies blow
Between the crosses, row on row,
That mark our place; and in the sky
The larks, still bravely singing, fly
Scarce heard amid the guns below.

We are the Dead. Short days ago
We lived, felt dawn, saw sunset glow,
Loved and were loved, and now we lie
In Flanders fields.

Take up our quarrel with the foe:
To you from failing hands we throw
The torch; be yours to hold it high.
If ye break faith with us who die
We shall not sleep, though poppies grow
In Flanders fields.

In order to practice, try recording yourself reciting the poem, and then practise playing the Underscore along to the recording. If possible, try to get a friend (or several friends) to read the poem whilst you accompany them, so you can practice making it fit a variety of different interpretations.

Further study

Try working through the following passages of Underscore, ideally with someone reading the dialogue.

- Underscore into "Perfectly Marvellous" (Cabaret)
- Underscore in the middle of "Long Ago" (Half a Sixpence)
- Underscore sections in "Being Alive" (Company)

CONDUCTING SHORTHAND

When preparing your conductor's score, you should think about the technicalities of conducting and set how you will beat the music. Practise conducting through the show (ideally cover to cover), to ensure you know exactly which beat patterns you are using. This process is important to Musical Directors of all experience as we are in an age where rehearsal time is costly, so it is essential to avoid any time-wasting in the rehearsal room ("how shall I conduct that *rall.*?" or "at what point shall I sub-divide into 8?" for example). "Mark up" your scores prior to rehearsals. This can be done in pencil or with a coloured pencil/pen (red is probably the most commonly used colour), so that it stands out when you glance down at the score.

A conventional shorthand for the various different beat patterns is as follows:

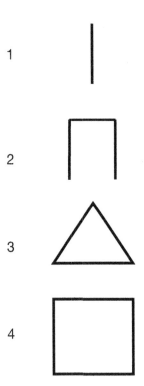

If you want to indicate a sub-divided beat (i.e. a bar of 4 which you will beat in 8) this can be shown as follows:

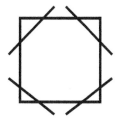

You can also use these symbols to indicate the division of the *strong musical beats* within the bar. For example, a bar of 5/8 can be subdivided one of two ways: either [2+3] (i.e. **1** 2 3 4 5) *or* [3+2] (i.e. **1** 2 3 **4** 5).

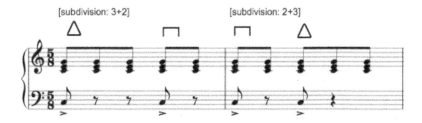

PLAN YOUR COUNT-INS

Think about how you will start each number. In more traditional Musicals where the music is rooted in classical music styles (such as "My Fair Lady" or "Les Miserables"), giving an up-beat into the start of each number would normally be appropriate. When conducting a groove-based show (such as "The Wedding Singer" or "Rent"), where the feel is rooted in contemporary pop and rock styles, it is common practice to give a count into the number ("count-in" or "counting off") i.e. "3,4..", "2,3,4..." or even "1,2,3,4..". When the rhythm section of the band is functioning more like a rock/pop band, a "1,2,3,4" count will ensure that the musicians start solidly together, and that they lock into the groove from beat 1. At other times, when you are conducting more *rubato* passages or *colla voce* sections, a "1,2,3,4" count will waste valuable time and energy, and an up-beat will be perfectly adequate. Shows that have a variety of musical styles, such as "Company" or "The Witches of Eastwick" may require a mix of "up-beats" and "count-ins" depending on the feel of the number (and sometimes the orchestra/band you are working with), so you should consider what you feel is appropriate number-by-number when preparing the score for rehearsals.

There may be times when the Deputy Stage Manager or Stage Manager who is "calling" the show will ask for a longer count so they can time a technical cue with the music, such as a lighting (LX) change, or change of scene/scenery. For example, a cloth flies out as the music starts, so in order to prepare the stage crew to fly the cloth, the person calling the show may ask you for a "3,4" count as opposed to just an up-beat. It is always helpful for you to know if any technical cues are being taken from your conducting so you can take extra care to make them clear.

"Calling" the show – The Stage Manager or Deputy Stage Manager will be positioned in Prompt Corner (an assigned place in either wing), giving cues to Sound, Stage Crew, Lighting and sometimes the Musical Director via "Cans" (a remote headphone system) or via cue lights. They are also responsible for calling the cast down to the stage in time for their scenes/musical numbers. This whole process is referred to as "calling" the show.

Fail to prepare.... and prepare to fail!

Chapter 4: **Auditions**

Before the rehearsal process can get underway, you first need to assemble your cast. "Casting" is the process whereby the Production Team and Creative Team decide who is going to play the various roles. For some repertory and amateur/community theatre companies, the show may be cast internally, i.e.: with people who are already enrolled in the company, but most common casting scenarios involve auditions.

PRE-AUDITION PREPARATION

It is important that you are familiar with the script and score before you begin the audition process. If you have prepared the score as discussed in the previous chapter, you will already be familiar with the musical demands of each character, and what you need from the ensemble. If you are entering the audition process before you have had chance to fully prepare the score, you will need to do some groundwork before you are ready to sit on the audition panel. After all, it would be impossible to cast the show not knowing what it is that you are casting!

When you read through the script, make sure you have a notepad to hand so you can make notes on the characters. When you cast each role, his or her singing voice should match the character they are playing. For example, a nasty villain will ideally have a threatening "nasty" quality to their singing voice; in the same way that the a young princess will ideally sound light and youthful with a sweet tone.

Once you have made your character notes go through the Vocal Score and note down the ranges for each of the characters. If you are working on a semi-professional or professional production the Casting Director/Producers may ask you to prepare a casting breakdown prior to the auditions. This will include all of the information about what type of person you are looking for.

Female Actress Required:

Playing age – 18-22 to play the role of "Princess Sparkle" in a new touring production of "Princess Sparkle and the Magic Kingdom". December 2012-February 2013.

Equity rates apply.

Mezzo Soprano (contemporary vocal qualities). Must be able to belt up to a D. Please prepare an up-tempo pop song and a contemporary Musical Theatre ballad.

As the Musical Director you will be expected to know the type of singers you are hoping to find from the audition process. Together with the Director, Choreographer (and Casting Director), you will make choices about who is best suited to the role, and who you think will be a good Company member.

THE AUDITION PROCESS

Audition processes vary in length depending on the size of production and the amount of time you have to cast it. In Amateur/Community theatre the auditions may take place on a Sunday afternoon, or perhaps one evening, in the rehearsal hall. However, if you are casting a large-scale professional production the process will normally take around 3 to 5 weeks. Once the auditions have taken place, the Producers will sit down with the creative team (Director, Choreographer, Musical Director and Casting Director) to make their decisions. On a professional or semi-professional production the offers will then be made (either directly to the actor or via their agent), and you then have to wait to see if the offers are accepted. On larger productions you would generally have a list of 1st, 2nd and 3rd reserves in case your first choice declines the offer. In an amateur dramatic/community/youth theatre production the casting may be announced at the next meeting/rehearsal, or via post/email in the weeks following the auditions.

It is common practice to have "set material" for auditions (normally sections of songs taken from the show you are casting). This will either be handed out before the auditions (where there is only one round) or at/after the 1st audition - to be prepared for the recall/2nd round. The auditionees are then expected to prepare the set material, with you and the Director giving them notes at their recalls on how to improve. It is vital that the artistic team uses the audition process to fully explore the auditionees, to make sure the correct casting decisions are ultimately made.

- During the audition process make sure you are confident that the singer has the range needed to play the role, and they can consistently reach the technical level that the role demands.
- Talk to the Director and Choreographer to make sure they agree with your choices. It is pointless having a great singer who can't act, or one who has two left feet. Equally, avoid engaging anyone who can't sing to the standard you require.
- Make sure that your notes to the auditionees are clear, unambiguous and constructive. "There were some wrong notes" is not helpful if you don't tell them which notes need correcting!
- Make sure you have the ranges for each character written down in the audition room so you can refer to these as necessary. For example: "PRINCE CHARMING" – High Baritone (Bottom G to F above middle C in full voice, good falsetto) "FAIRY QUEEN" – Mezzo Soprano. Belt up to a C#, must have a sweet head voice (up to top A)
- Plan which sections of the score you would like the various characters to prepare for the recalls. Ensure you are covering the "big" moments, and include exposed solos or tricky bits that need to be explored.
- Auditions are a nerve-racking experience for everyone involved. Whether or not someone is a "good singer", you should respect the fact that they have taken time to come and sing for you, and always listen to them respectfully and attentively.

> Casting Director - The Casting Director is the person responsible for assembling the cast for a show. They will initially prepare a shortlist of audition candidates (based on the criteria set out by the creative team). Although the Artistic team will ultimately make the decisions, the Casting Director will then be present throughout the audition process to advise and help with the casting.

AUDITION NOTES

It is common practice to use an audition sheet for each candidate. The panel will make notes on the auditionee on this sheet (in each discipline). For example:

L.S. Casting
London

"Oklahoma" UK Tour 2013

Name: Joe Bloggs
Agent: ASA
Phone Number: 020 1111 1111

ACTING	SINGING	MOVEMENT	OTHER
Good Scene, took notes and direction well. Well prepared	Top Tenor Nice, warm vocal qualities. Range? Good strong belt. Explore in recall...	Trained dancer, nice style and good body. B+	Good vibe, friendly

- Make clear and concise notes on each candidate so that you and the team can refer to them at a later stage. For example, voice type (Soprano/Alto/Tenor/Bass) or range; a note on the "quality" of the voice (full and rich, warm, soft, breathy, husky etc.); general "vibe" (friendly, confident, abrupt, serious, unprepared etc.) Always make sure your notes are helpful, never personal or rude.

You may be asked to grade the auditionees (this is common practice in Dance auditions where the groups are large and it would be impractical to write copious notes on each individual). Grading systems are useful when you are looking back through the notes in order to make your final casting decisions. The grade may either take the form of a number system (e.g.: 7/10, 5/10....) or a letter system (C+, A- etc....)

- If you use a grading system make sure it is consistent, especially if the auditions are spread over several days. Set personal criteria for your grading scheme, and write it down if necessary so you can refer back to it.

AUDITION PIANISTS

Depending on budget and personal preference, you may decide to work with an audition pianist. Some Directors prefer to have the Musical Director sitting next to them so they can discuss each candidate without the distraction of them accompanying. However, others will be happy for the Musical Director to play for the auditions themselves. Your personal preference will probably depend on your own piano skills, and your sight-reading ability.

Another way of working is to have an audition pianist for the 1st round of auditions when the candidates are bringing in their own songs (thus eliminating the need for you to sight-read), and later with you as the Musical Director playing for the recall round(s). This method can be effective if you plan to work through material with the candidates around the piano, as it will be quicker for you to play it yourself rather than explaining everything to the pianist (i.e.: finding the right bar to start from, try this bit again, take it up a tone etc..). If there is an Assistant Musical Director on board they will sometimes be expected to play for auditions.

Whatever method you decide upon, if you are working with an Audition Pianist you must make sure you look after them. It is a stressful job playing for auditions (something I feel every Musical Director should experience for themselves at some point), and it can be made much harder with a difficult Musical Director breathing down their neck.

YOUR BEST 16 BARS PLEASE....

Depending on the time frame available, you will sometimes only have time to listen to "16 bars". This doesn't literally mean 16 bars, but really means just a short verse and chorus, or perhaps just a chorus (depending on the tempo) to give the audition panel an idea of the voice (i.e. Is it in tune? Vocal quality? Style?) If you are auditioning dancers (who are primarily *dancers* who sing, as opposed to *singers* who dance), you may just ask for them to sing 16 bars after their dance audition, or time permitting, a verse and chorus (around 32 bars).

Sometimes a show will have "open" auditions. This means that there won't be any pre-allocated time slots for each auditionee and everyone just turns up and waits until it is their turn to sing. Because open auditions are generally busy, and the standard can vary greatly (as literally *anyone* can turn up), the criteria for these is generally "turn up with your best 16 bars". If the 16 bars sound good, and the person fits the casting criteria, you would ask the person to stay and sing more of the song, or come back for a recall at a later date.

A typical audition schedule for a large-scale professional production

Week 1:
Monday-Friday   **10:30-5:00**   **1st round auditions**

- *A list of suitable auditionees is put together by the Casting Director based on the criteria set out by the Artistic Team. The candidates turn up to sing their own song for the Audition Panel. Each audition will last for around 5 minutes.*

Week 2:

Monday-Friday	10:30-5:00	1st rounds/1st recalls

- A mixed week of more 1st round auditions, and some recalls from the 1st week. The recalls will be based around the material (audition pack) that has been sent to those who made it through the 1st round, and will normally include some music, and some scenes or sections of scenes. Each recall audition will last 5-10 minutes.

Week 3:

Monday & Tuesday	10:00-11:30/ 12:00-13:30/ 14:00-15:30	Dance Auditions (separate sessions for boys and girls)
Wed-Fri	10:30-5:00	1st recalls/2nd recalls

- Dance auditions at the start of the week. These will normally take the form of a group audition (groups between 10 and 75), and the day will be divided into sessions. Those who are successful in the dance rounds will be asked to stay to sing at the end of the session, or the end of the day. The rest of the week will be a mix of 1st and 2nd recalls.

Week 4:

Monday	10:00-12:00/ 13:00-15:00	Dance Recalls (incl. singing auditions)
Tuesday-Friday	10:30-5:00	2nd recalls/3rd recalls

- One afternoon session in week 4 will probably include a movement call for those singers who have successfully made it through 3 recalls. This is to ensure that they are able to take movement direction and/or pick up basic choreography.

Week 5:

One day	10:00-end	Final Auditions

- The final audition (or "Finals" as they are often known) will normally be in front of an extended panel that may include the senior Artistic/Creative Team (Music Supervisor & Writers) and the Producers, alongside the audition panel from the earlier rounds. It is normally followed by a casting meeting where the decisions on who to make job offers to will be made.

This is a typical outline of the audition timetable for a large scale Musical with a large cast (up to 40+ people). If the cast is smaller, or the budget is limited, this process may be condensed to 2 or 3 weeks, or sometimes less depending on the Producer. For semi-professional and community/amateur dramatic shows there may be only one round of dance auditions and acting/singing auditions.

Mr. & Mrs. Nice

Make sure you're always approachable, fair and supportive in auditions. The "X-Factor" style audition is as much about making good TV as it is about finding talent. There is no place in theatre for Simon Cowell-style Musical Directors!

₩Chapter 5: **In the rehearsal room**

Once you have assembled your cast, you will be ready to start rehearsals. In Amateur Dramatic and Community Theatre productions you may dive into the rehearsal period immediately after the auditions (sometimes the following week or weekend), whereas in professional productions there will normally be a period after the auditions where contracts are agreed before you embark on the rehearsal process. In professional theatre this process can take anything from two or three weeks up to several months.

₩orking with the Cast

THE FIRST REHEARSAL

The rehearsal room on the first day of any rehearsal process will be filled with a variety of emotions. There is always a level of excitement when starting a new show and meeting the people you'll be working with. The room will also be filled with a nervous energy; invariably, most people will have been through a potentially stressful audition process, and now they are in the show, they have to prove that they can deliver the goods! As well as **the Cast**, you can expect to see **the Director, Choreographer,** a representative from the **Production team**, and members of **Stage Management** at the first rehearsal. The Orchestra will not be present until much later in the process (normally at the [first] Band Call), and they won't meet the cast properly until the *Sitzprobe* or *Wandelprobe* (more on these later). On larger shows, members of the **Wardrobe** department may also attend, and sometimes the **Designers** (Set, Lighting and Sound) and **Writers** may also be in attendance on the first day.

To begin with (after a *meet and greet* over a cup of tea) you will normally go round the room so that everyone can introduce themselves. You may feel an enormous weight on your shoulders as you introduce yourself as the Musical Director for the first time;

after all, you are responsible for all aspects of the music in performance - and that responsibility must never be taken lightly!

If you are rehearsing a "book show" (i.e. a show that has a story and a script, as opposed to a *Variety* or compilation show), there will normally be a read through of the script at the first rehearsal. As the Musical Director you may be asked to play <u>and sing</u> the songs as you get to them in the read through. It is certainly worth practicing this in advance to make sure you won't be caught out! The rest of the room will not expect you to be the world's greatest singer, but it is important that you are comfortable belting it out "loud and proud", so people can hear the tunes and get the general idea of the feel of the score.

- Make sure you know the tempos. Don't be caught out trying to guess the speed of a number or showing any kind of uncertainty in front of the cast.
- Speak to the Director and Choreographer before hand about the dance breaks/routines, to discuss how much or how little of the dance breaks are required at the read through. It is often not necessary to play extensive dance music in a read through, but equally you may sometimes be asked to give an edited "flavour" of a dance section for everyone to hear.

The read through will normally be followed by a vocal rehearsal (vocal call) with the full company, so you should think about what you are going to teach at this rehearsal. Depending on the show you may decide <u>not</u> to start at the beginning. For example, if you are mounting a production of "Oklahoma" it may be a good idea to have a good sing of the title number on the first day (even though this song appears in the latter part of Act 2). In this way, you are teaching a company number that involves everyone, and none of the cast are left redundant. If you were to work chronologically on this particular show, you would have everyone sitting around doing nothing as the ensemble don't sing until Act 1:number 8. Wherever possible, try to involve everyone in your first full company rehearsal, and make sure you end the rehearsal on a high, sending everyone home feeling good about the show, and also feeling good about themselves. (On this occasion, the *very beginning* wouldn't be a *very good place to start!*)

- Plan the number that you will be teaching (i.e.: how you will teach it, where the breath points will be, any diction issues, how the harmonies are divided, accents, phrasing and interpretation as discussed in Chapter 3).
- Give yourself enough time to finish with a sing through of whatever you learn, and try to pick something that will sound good when you sing it through at the end. This will help to keep morale high and make everyone excited about coming back for the second rehearsal.
- Plan how the harmonies will be split/broken down (e.g.: SATB, Mixed Voices, Male/Female etc...). Avoid the "how shall we divide this chord up, then?!" moment. It is important you come across as organized, decisive and confident.

It is often a good idea to look through the score number-by-number to work out how to divide up the Cast/Company (e.g. SATB, Male/Female, 3 mixed parts etc...) and then write it down either on a grid/chart, or in your Piano/Conductor score (either on the index/contents page, or on the 1st page of each number in the Score). For some shows it will be clearly marked in, but commonly (especially with modern Musicals) there will be an element of de-coding to be done, and some important choices for you to make about how harmonies should be divided up.

LEARNING NAMES

Personally, I have a shocking memory for names, so I always try to learn as many names as possible in advance of the first day of rehearsals. If you have a great memory for names you can ignore this paragraph. If not, then please read on! If you have been on the audition panel, you will hopefully remember some names. Equally, if you are reading this as a school teacher, or someone who has worked with a particular group before, you will already know most (or all) of the names of the cast. If it is a new group, and you're not familiar with everyone's names, it is important that you learn them quickly, early on in the rehearsal process if possible. "Darling", "love" and "mate" count for a lot in theatre when it comes to remembering names, but are not so helpful when it comes to noting individuals during rehearsals or in performance.

At the first vocal rehearsal, I ask the cast to sit in their parts, and then I tell them I'm awful at learning names, so can they sit in the same places for the first week's rehearsals until I learn them all! I then quickly write down the names on a piece of paper, which I keep on top of the piano and then make a point of using their names as much as possible during the rehearsals.

For example:

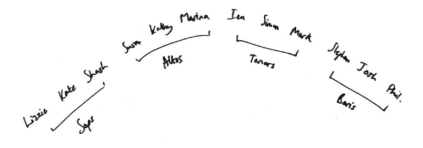

I decided early on that I found it hard learning names, and ultimately gave up trying. I quickly came un-stuck when the Director asked me a question such as "How's Lizzie doing with her harmonies?" and when the Sound Operator asked "which of the Tenors is the strongest?" and "who's microphone is sticking out in the mix?" This was the point when I realised I needed to stop being so lazy! I've found that having a name grid on the piano for the first week works for me. You may have your own method that works best for you. Whatever method you choose to use, it's important that you learn the names of the whole company, as well as the names of key members of the crew (stage management, sound team, lighting etc.)

VOCAL WARM UP

Wherever possible, you should begin your rehearsals with a vocal warm-up. Like other muscles in the body, the muscles of the voice need stretching and warming up before they will work effectively. You wouldn't go for a twenty mile run without warming up first, so in the same way you shouldn't launch into a three hour singing call without first warming up the voice. A group vocal warm up is also a time to bring the company together to sing, and a time for them to bond as a group. I am aware that some Musical Directors and performers don't agree with a company warm up as they either feel that it is impossible to warm the voice up in 10-15 minutes, or indeed as you have been already talking throughout the day prior to the rehearsal, your voice is already sufficiently warmed up. I personally disagree with both of these points as I can (and do) work the entire vocal range, as well as going through the different vocal qualities in 10-15 minutes, and I am yet to meet anyone who talks at the extremes of the vocal range covered in a warm up; I therefore don't see how you can warm up your whole range just by talking!

PLANNING YOUR WARM UP

You should plan your vocal warm up to ensure that you cover the necessary range and vocal timbres. Start in a lower register, where the muscles are in a more neutral and relaxed state, and work your way up into the higher registers. Scales are good for this as they gradually stretch and warm up the muscles as you work your way up the scale. Regularly remind the Company not to force their voices up to notes that they are not comfortable with, and encourage them to drop out or jump down the octave if it gets too high.

You should also use some exercises in your warm up that work the articulators (the muscles of the lips and tongue). Tongue twisters can be fun and work well as warm ups.

Try to explore the different voice qualities in your warm up, i.e.: thin and thick folds ("head" and "chest" voice), "classical"-tilted sounds, belting (take extra care with belting), loud and soft, high and low, long legato lines and quick energized exercises. If possible speak to an experienced singing teacher, so they can describe what the singing muscles are, and advise the best ways to warm them up (also see notes in Chapter 2).

- A word of caution: always take care when warming up the voice, and when asking singers to sing in specific ways. Learn about the voice first, and never ask a singer (or ensemble) to do anything that is unsafe and will hurt their voices.

Below are several examples of the type of exercise you could use as part of your vocal warm up.

- The first exercise is gentle, to focus the group and begin stretching the muscles.
- The second exercise covers a much wider range, and encourages long phrases and good breath control.
- The third exercise gets the mouth, lips and tongue working in a nice vocal *agility* warm up.
- The fourth exercise is a tongue twister, useful for warming up the different muscles in the mouth (and the brain) - and it's also quite good fun!
- The fifth exercise is a "warm-up standard" in the West End theatre world. It covers a wide range, and encourages long phrases and good breath control.

Familiar songs that gradually work up a scale, or which are useful as phrasing exercises are also great to use as part of a vocal warm up. Some common examples are the opening phrases of "The Way You Look Tonight", "Somewhere over the rainbow" and "Bali Ha'i".

Varying your warm ups

If you are working with a cast for a period of time try to vary your vocal warm ups. If you are not careful (when a show has been running for a long time) vocal warm ups can degenerate into a little social time with lots of talking and not so much warming up! If you vary your warm ups and try to keep them interesting (challenging the cast with some new tongue twisters or trying out some more rhythmically tricky exercises), you will stand more chance of holding the interest, and more chance of the cast actually warming up their voices! (There are several good books with suggestions for vocal warm ups – see appendix for details).

There's a chip shop in space sell-ingspace ship shaped chips, There's a chip shop in space sell-ing

space ship shaped chips, There's a chip shop in space sell - ing...

There are lots of different tongue twisters out there to try. You can either sing them to a major scale, or perhaps try writing a tune to go with them.

Bel - la Sen - or - a

Bel - la Sen - or - a

Continue up to Ab major. *Note:* Singers who are familiar with this will often harmonise as they sing.

REHEARSING THE CAST

Here are a few thoughts on rehearsing the Cast:

- Encourage the singers to record their harmony lines onto a Dictaphone or digital voice recorder. They can then use these recordings to practice in their own time, and will then have a copy of their harmonies to refer to at any point leading up to the performance(s).

- Wherever possible give the cast musical scores (i.e. written out vocal parts or copies of the Piano/Vocal score) rather than working from lyric sheets (i.e. the words/lyrics typed up with no music). This way, you can refer to bar numbers and the cast can see the contours of the vocal line (even if they cannot read music), and where the vocal lines and harmonies divide up. Using sheet music will also encourage those who don't read music to develop these skills.

- Be specific about breath-points, bring offs, diction and pronunciation (as discussed in Chapter 3) and avoid being vague when you are rehearsing. For example: "hold that note for quite a long time, then make sure you come off together" is not helpful to a cast. "Hold for 5 beats, come off on beat 6 with a nice, strong 't'" is clear and leaves no room for ambiguity. Encourage the cast to mark everything in their scores and to bring their scores to every rehearsal. Markings should always be done in pencil rather than pen so they can be altered if necessary.

- Be strict with yourself and others about time keeping. Everyone's time is precious, and it is disrespectful to all involved if time is wasted. Start and finish on time. Don't spend too long talking and philosophizing about things that are irrelevant to the show as this only wastes valuable rehearsal time. Avoid being the Musical Director who loves the sound of their own voice. Use your time wisely and plan your rehearsals well.

TEACHING HARMONIES

When you are teaching harmonies, break down the harmonies slowly and systematically, allowing yourself plenty of rehearsal time to do this. If you rush through the teaching process you will invariably end up losing people along the way, and group morale will suffer as a result. It is important when you are teaching harmonies not to let the group think the music is too difficult for them, especially if the harmonies are quite complex. There is a big difference between stretching a group (and them knowing that this is what you are doing) and making them feel that they are just not good enough. It is important that you tell the group when they are doing well and when it sounds good, as well as letting them know when it is wrong and needs correcting.

- Start by playing through the harmony lines at the piano in manageable sections (eight or sixteen bar phrases).
- When working with younger children and teenagers they often find it helpful if you sing their lines whilst you play them (at pitch, if possible.) This will encourage them to sing along, and they will subliminally pick up your intended phrasing from the way you sing it.
- Play/sing each harmony line twice before asking the group to sing back the line a further two times (or more, if they are struggling to pick it up).
- Once you have taught and run each harmony line and you are confident they have picked it up, try running the different harmony lines all together. If the music is particularly complicated, perhaps try running different combinations of harmony lines (e.g. "let's hear the Tenors and Sopranos together once), and during this process highlight any areas of difficulty such as tricky intervals, close counterpoint, and deliberate clashes in the writing.
- Tell the singers how to find their starting note. It can often be related to the passage of music which comes directly before; e.g. "Altos start on the same note as the solo line finishes on", or "Tenors go down a fourth from the end of the clarinet instrumental that comes before this section". You could always use the "famous" interval examples listed in Chapter 3 to aid this process.

For example, if you were teaching the following passage of music, you could help the Tenors by telling them that their harmony note for "little" is the same note they began with on the first "twinkle".

You could tell the Altos that they go *down* from the second "twinkle" for their harmony note for "little", and you could tell any Sopranos who don't know the melody that they go *up* to their note for "little" after the second "twinkle". And so on.

Soprano/
Alto

Twin - kle, twin - kle   lit - tle   star,   how   I   won - der   what you are.

Tenors

mp dolce semplice

Never be afraid to state the obvious. Sometimes things which are crystal clear to you (as someone who can read music proficiently) will not be apparent to a singer who doesn't read music, or to someone who is inexperienced in singing harmonies.

- Give yourself plenty of time to teach harmony lines. Avoid rushing through them as this will only worry the singers, and you will end up having to go through it all again at a later date.
- Play and sing through each harmony line yourself *before* you teach it. This way, you can highlight any tricky passages *before* you teach them to the cast.

Whilst you will normally sit the singers in their parts during the early rehearsals (i.e.: Soprano, Altos, Tenors, and Bartitones), it is useful to jumble everyone up later in the rehearsal process, so singers end up sitting next to someone who is singing a different part. As well as being a great way to check how secure individuals are with their harmony lines, it is also a good preparatory exercise for when the Company stage the numbers, as it is very rare that each harmony group will be standing and moving together in harmony groups on stage.

Rounds and Canons

When working with singers who are not used to singing in harmony, why not try singing some Rounds and Canons* first, as a way to introduce harmony singing and counterpoint. This will help to get the group used to singing different lines at the same time. There are lots of Rounds and Canons to try, and these can also be used as part of your warm-up process (and as "ice-breakers" in your first sessions).

*Banana Splits, compiled by Ana Sanderson (A&C Black) has lots of great canons and rounds to try out.

Ooo Ah!

When you are teaching vocal lines that don't contain lyrics such as passages of "ooos" and "ahs", you should explain to the cast the context of the music so that they can perform them in the correct dramatic context. Just because they aren't singing lyrics it doesn't mean that there is no meaning behind what they are singing. You will rarely find "ooos" and "ahs" simply because they *sound nice*. Often a composer or arranger will add backing vocals to heighten the drama. For this reason, you should encourage the cast to read the lyrics that are being sung alongside their "ooos" and "ahs", to create an understanding of what they are portraying through the music.

This is also true when there are passages with musical interjections from the Ensemble. For example, if a performer sings "that was amazing!" and the ensemble echoes the "amazing!" immediately after, this can be likened to an evangelical Preacher saying something profound, and the congregation repeating the key word(s) spontaneously as a way of agreeing and acknowledging it. There are also times when the ensemble joins in to sing the choruses. Again, this is a device used by Composers and Arrangers to heighten the drama, whilst expanding the tonal colour, to create a unified wall of sound that can be a powerful way to convey the lyrics.

Always take time in rehearsals to ensure that everyone understands the meaning behind what they are singing; be it a straightforward lyric, or other sounds such as "oohs", "ah's", "oh's" or humming.

PLANNING YOUR REHEARSALS

Think ahead at the start of the rehearsal process to the amount of time that you have to teach the score, and plan how you will achieve this in the allocated rehearsal time. The Director will normally be responsible for the rehearsal schedules (in liaison with the Choreographer and yourself.) The Choreographer will often request that you teach the company numbers (songs involving the Ensemble and Full Company) in the same, or similar order to how they will be staged/choreographed. It will help the Choreographer if you teach the "dance" numbers (i.e. songs having a large choreographic element) first. It is easier for them to teach the choreography if the dancers are familiar with the song as certain elements of the choreography will link to specific lyrics and set points in the music.

Once you know how many rehearsal sessions there will be, you can work out how much time you have to teach the songs. Your music calls will either be Full Company rehearsals (where you can work on the group/ensemble numbers) or solo/individual vocal calls (where you work with the principals/soloists).

- Plan your rehearsals **in advance** to avoid company members attending rehearsals and then sitting around doing nothing. Make lists of who is in each number, so you can see which members of the Company will be needed number-by-number, and add this to the rehearsal schedule.
- When working on solos/duets/trios, make sure that you decide which numbers will be worked on in the session, and have this added to the rehearsal call so the cast know what they need to prepare in advance of the rehearsal.

Once you know how much time you have, make up a rough plan of how long you have to teach each number. For example, if there are six Company numbers in the show and you have 3x3hour rehearsals, this works out at 1½ hours per number. If only it were that simple! Perhaps two of these six numbers are vocally quite complex (venturing into six-part harmony), whereas three of the numbers are relatively simple (SATB) and one is just some unison "ooos" and "ahs". Maybe you should allow one and a half hours for each of the complex numbers, and a further half hour to clean each of them (at a later session) and then one hour for each of the other three SATB numbers and a further fifteen minutes clean up on each, thirty minutes to teach the simple unison number, and thirty minutes (in the last session) to sing through all six numbers in show running order. This is perhaps a more realistic plan, although without being too specific (i.e.: knowing the show, the specific Musical Director's teaching method and knowing the ability and focus of the Company), it is difficult to prescribe a categorical rehearsal plan. The main thing to remember when planning your rehearsals is to **be realistic**. Don't try to cram so much in to a rehearsal that everyone leaves feeling brain-fried and nervous about coming back; but equally, don't spend hours talking about the music and constantly going over the same section, so everyone ends up feeling rather bored!

Professional Production:

HALF A SIXPENCE
Lyric Theatre

Wednesday 16th October

Pineapple Studio 2	Pineapple Studio 6
10:30 - "Flash Bang Wallop" (Full Ensemble)	11:30 - "I know what I am" Miss James
12:30 - Mr John to join	12:15 - "Half a Sixpence"/ "Long Ago" Mr Stephenson to join
13:30 - Lunch	
14:30 - "Old Military Canal" (Full ensemble)	13:30 - Lunch
17:30 - Call Ends	14:30 - Act 1-Scene1 Act 2, Scene 5 Miss James, Mr Stephenson
	18:00 - Call Ends

Youth Theatre Production:

Millfield Youth Theatre

Sunday 10th September

13:30	"Little Shop of Horrors" (Stuart) Lauren, Frances and Robyn "Cell Block Tango" (Lizzie) Ronnie, Bianca, Georgina, Charlotte N, Lydia, Tamara
14:30	Dance Warm Up (Full Company)
14:45	Vocal Warm Up (Full Company)
15:00	Grease (Lizzie) A Chorus Line (Stuart)
15:45	Grease (Stuart) A Chorus Line (Lizzie)
16:15	Break
16:30	Rhythm of Life
17:10	You Can't Stop The Beat
17:30	Finish

- Notice how the Youth Theatre rehearsal schedule covers lots of different material, and works in short sections. As they meet on a weekly basis (as opposed to a professional Company who would usually work Monday-Saturday), working in short sections helps to keep lots of different material fresh in the mind, and helps to keep the energy level up in the rehearsal room, with no time to get bored working on one particular number.

- Note, also, the difference in the rehearsal times for each of the example schedules. A Community Theatre Company, Amateur Dramatic Company or Youth Theatre Company will normally work on a weekend or a week day evening, far from the conventional Monday-Friday daytime working hours; a professional Company will normally rehearse Monday-Saturday 10:30-6:00 (sometimes 9:00 or 10:00-18:30 or 19:00).

OVER-REHEARSING

As the conscientious Musical Director, you will, no doubt, want to rehearse the show to the point where it feels safe and secure, where you feel confident that it will be musically solid once it reaches the performance stage. In striving to achieve this ideal you must take care not to over-rehearse. This will only lead to boredom with the singing sounding stale and under-energized.

Many will agree that one of the best aspects of working on a show is the adrenaline rush you feel upon the opening night, and hopefully at every performance thereafter! If the show is over-rehearsed, this adrenaline rush will be substantially reduced because the cast will be bored singing the same songs and dancing the same routines, and the nervous energy that accompanies the excitement of performance will not be there. This can also happen when you add the elements associated with performance too early in the rehearsal process. The excitement the cast feel when they hear the Orchestra for the first time wouldn't be there if the Orchestra were present throughout the entire rehearsal process (this can be the danger of using backing tracks for both rehearsal and performance). In the same way, if you had costumes, full make up and performance lighting for every rehearsal from the start, there would be no excitement when putting them on for the dress rehearsal. If the lighting, make-up, costumes, scenery and Orchestra are added towards the end of the rehearsal process, it gives the cast a final lift to take them into the performances.

The other danger of over rehearsing is the complacency that can start to develop as the cast become over-familiar with the show. This, in turn, will lead to people making silly mistakes, and ultimately giving a "sparkle free", slightly jaded opening night!

KEEPING IN TOUCH WITH THE TEAM

Teamwork is vital when mounting a theatrical production, and communication is the key to a successful Artistic Team.

- Speak to the rest of the Artistic Team at the end of each rehearsal. Discuss the rehearsal you have just taken, and make a plan of how to approach the next session. Discuss any issues or problems that may have arisen in the rehearsal, and identify anything which needs sorting out before the next time you meet.

If you have a Stage Manager working with you, make sure you keep in touch with them too. Let them know your needs, and remember too that they have lots of other jobs to do as well as looking after you! The days when the "grand" Musical Director walks into a room and demands that someone gets them a coffee with milk and two sugars have long gone! Also, it is not fair to walk into rehearsals five minutes before they begin and demand that the room is re-set, or you want an extra table, a different piano stool, a bigger music stand etc. Make sure you put in your requests to the Stage Management team in adequate time for them to fulfil your needs.

MARRYING THE TEXT AND MUSIC

We have already discussed the importance of looking at the meaning of the lyrics and the idea of the music being integrated into the script. During the rehearsal process, alongside the singing and dancing rehearsals there will be acting calls, where the Director will work with the actors on their scenes. If the scene contains a song, you should try to be present as the actors rehearse that scene, not necessarily to accompany the rehearsal on piano (although you may choose to do so), but rather to listen to the Director's comments about the shape of the scene and the journey of the character, to ensure that the character development continues through the music and the song is integrated into the scene(s) around it.

- If the Actors are using a specific *voice quality* for the preceding scene, make sure there is no perceptible change in vocal quality as they move into the song (unless it is for specific dramatic reasons). For example, if the cue line is spoken gently and the opening music is soft, make sure the voice has the same *resonance* and *colour* as it did in the preceding scene, such that the drama can flow from the scene into the music. Conversely, if there is an argument in the preceding scene that continues into the song make sure the vocal tone doesn't become lyrical and indulgent as the actor begins to sing. Encourage actors to keep the *edge* in the vocal tone so it still sounds like an argument, thus allowing the song to seamlessly flow from the scene.

Always let the drama lead the music - never the other way around.

WORKING WITH CHOREOGRAPHERS & DANCERS

The first thing to note when working with Choreographers and Dancers is that they normally work in counts of "eights" and not in bars. If you are working in a moderate 4/4 time signature, a dancer's "8" will probably mean 2 bars. If it is a fast "4" you may find yourself being asked "how many eights is that?" and "are they slow or fast eights?" The easiest way to work it out is to count your "eights" out loud. The most comfortable way to count will often be the one that the Choreographer and Dancers are using. If it becomes a tongue twister to count eights as crotchets in a fast 4/4, then you are probably right to assume they will be counting in "slow eights" and that these will be minims/half notes – hence one lot of "eight" will be equivalent to 4 bars. When you are working in waltz time (or any other music in triple meter) the count of "eights" will probably be counted as one bar per count, so one "eight" would be 8 bars.

Have a look at the following examples. The counts above the stave indicate the dancers counts:

(Note how in the first example the 2nd lot of 8 starts with a "2". This is common practice amongst dancers and choreographers. The third lot would therefore be "<u>3</u> 2 3 4 5 6 7 8" continuing up to "<u>8</u> 2 3 4 5 6 7 8")

When you are accompanying dance rehearsals (or "dance calls" as they are often known), either as a rehearsal pianist, Assistant Musical Director or as the Musical Director, try to keep a close eye on what is happening choreographically. When Choreographers are creating new routines they will expect you to be aware of where they are in the music. It is important that you don't hold up the rehearsal because you weren't paying attention and can't find which bar to pick up from. You should also be able to accompany sections of choreography without any confusion. For these reasons it is helpful to make pencil notes on your score that identify where the "hits" are (as in "jump" on beat 4 of bar 22 etc...). The more knowledgeable of dance terminology you are, the easier this process becomes.

- Always take an interest in the dance/choreography. Your relationship with the Choreographer and Dance Captain is an important one. The more appreciative you are of the dance, the more your conducting will compliment the routines in performance.
- When you are rehearsing with Dancers and they are running sections, they will normally work to a count-in. The most common count-in is "5,6,7,8". It will either be the Choreographer, Dance Captain or you that gives the count, so if it falls to you, make sure it is loud and clear, and also at the same tempo they have just been rehearsing at. It is worth noting that dancers often work under-tempo when learning routines, so make sure you are constantly monitoring the tempo and noting it accordingly.

USING A METRONOME

When working with Dancers, it is important to keep your tempi consistent. Don't be afraid to use a metronome for heavily dance-orientated numbers, both in rehearsal and in performance. If the Choreographer has planned their routine around a specific recording, make sure that your tempo matches the recording tempo otherwise it may disrupt the choreography. If you are not happy with the tempo of a specific recording that the Choreographer is working to, it is important to let them know as early in the process as possible, and then, ideally making them a new recording at the tempo that you are happy with, and which can be used in subsequent rehearsals (a piano recording should be more than adequate).

If you are working with a rehearsal pianist, you should also encourage them to use a metronome. Coffee, fatigue and adrenaline can affect our perception of tempi, so it is always advisable to refer to a metronome, even if only for confirmation. A few beats per minute (bpm) faster or slower could be crucial to the Dancers and Choreographer, even if it is imperceptible to most listeners.

FURTHERING YOUR DANCE KNOWLEDGE

It is helpful for all Musical Directors to have a good knowledge of different dance styles:

- Check out the following dances and listen to their inherent qualities:
  Tango, Waltz, Fox Trot, Polka, Shuffle, Beguine, Rumba, Quick Step

- Watch some examples of the following types of dancing so you have an awareness of the different styles:
  Ballet*, Street Jazz*, Modern, Contemporary, *Tap**.

  *These styles are commonly used in Musical Theatre

Get dancing...

The best way to further your dance knowledge is to head on down to a dance class and have a go yourself. As well as giving you a taster of what dancers go through, it will also give you a chance to put on your *boogie shoes* and bust out some moves!

RUNNING THE SHOW FOR THE FIRST TIME
IN THE REHEARSAL ROOM

You will normally run through the entire show with piano accompaniment in the rehearsal room, prior to moving into the theatre.

Depending on how the show has been rehearsed and the working practices of your colleagues, you may have already done a "put together" of sections of the show prior to the piano run-through (e.g. running scenes 1-3 in sequence including the dialogue, musical numbers and choreography). If this is the case you will already have a feel for how the different sections run together, and the first full run through may be smoother as a result. If you haven't had chance to run shorter sections prior to the first full run through, it may be slightly *stop-starty* - but it is nonetheless a worthwhile exercise. Make sure you are well prepared for the first run through, using this rehearsal to give yourself a clear picture of how well the cast are progressing and what areas need rehearsing/fixing.

- Check with the Director & Choreographer to decide whether or not to include the Overture in the run-through, or just the last section of it.
- Discuss any scene change music that may be required prior to the run, and then play it in the run to check the lengths are correct. If you are working on a new show and the scene change music has not yet been written, make sure that you have a stopwatch next to you so that you can time the scene changes in the run and then work out the music accordingly.
- Have a note pad to hand to make notes for yourself and the cast.
- Check that you have all of the cue lines and warning lines clearly marked in your script and score.
- Check that you know how you will count-in and conduct each number, so the cast and stage management team can become familiar with this.
- If you are doing a compilation show or a *Variety* Show, or are working from a Vocal Score/PC that you have assembled yourself, make sure your music is all in the correct order in a folder so you aren't hunting around for the correct piece of music.

WITH A NOTE PAD IN HAND....

Always keep a note pad to hand so you can write things down in the rehearsal room. There is nothing worse than getting home, or arriving at the following rehearsal thinking to yourself "I'm sure we changed something there, what was it?!" If you make notes, you can always refer back to them at a later date. Don't try to remember changes, splits, new routines, cuts etc. A wise teacher once told me "an amateur tries to remember, a professional writes it down!"*

* I am indebted to Dave Howson for this invaluable advice.

Working with the Orchestra

BOOKING THE ORCHESTRA

At some point either before or during the rehearsal period the musicians for the Orchestra/Band will need to be engaged. On smaller scale productions it will often be part of the Musical Director's duties to engage the musicians (or "fix", as it is commonly termed).

Here are a few things to keep in mind when booking the musicians:

- Double check the date and time of the rehearsals and performance before making any calls to the musicians.
- Prepare directions/maps on how to get to the rehearsal venue, and include any helpful information about transport links and parking.
- Check the orchestration and let the musicians know which instruments they need to bring. For example: does the guitarist need electric, acoustic guitars (steel or nylon) and/or banjo, and what (if any) special effects do they need, such as distortion, chorus etc.? What instruments do the reed players need, and if the parts include saxophones, which saxophones are required by each different player? (soprano, alto, tenor or baritone), which mutes do the brass players need (harmon, cup, straight, bucket, plunger), and what percussion instruments are written into the part? Is it a straight drum kit or does it need specific cymbals (splash, china, rivet), small hand-held percussion (such as triangle, woodblock, tambourine, finger cymbals, mark tree/wind chimes….), or does it require larger tuned percussion (such as timpani, glock, xylophone, vibraphone etc.)
- Let the musicians know about any fees and/expenses, and how this will be paid to them. Also clarify who they should be invoicing, when, and how (cheque, bank transfer, cash etc.) they should expect to receive any payments. The producing company may also ask you to advise the

musicians in writing that they are responsible for their own tax and/or National Insurance contributions.

- Clarify all rehearsal and performance times and also what the dress code is. This should all be done in a letter or email to avoid any confusion.
- Let the musicians know your policy on deputies. This will help to avoid any disagreements at a later date.

You may choose to engage your musicians by letter or via email. Either way, it is good to have **written** confirmation of the booking so that it can be referred back to at a later date, either by you or the musician. Avoid engaging musicians by text message, or by a third party as this is where confusion can creep in.

Here is an example of a letter, which may be used to engage a musician for an amateur operatic society show:

LOUTH OPERATIC SOCIETY

12a Pearsons Drive
Louth
Linconshire
LL1 1LN

Tel: 0777 777 777
yourname@email.com

12/02/2012

Dear Simon,

Further to our recent phone conversation I am writing with regard to the LOUTH OPERATIC SOCIETY forthcoming production of GUYS & DOLLS that you have kindly agreed to play for. Please note the following dates in your diary:

BAND CALL:
Sunday 14th March – 14:00-17:00
Louth Music Hall, 12 High Road, Louth LL1 LLN
Please bring a music stand to this rehearsal

TECHNICAL REHEARSAL:
Monday 15th March– 18:30-22:30
Louth New Theatre, Main Square, Louth LL2 LLM

DRESS REHEARSAL:
Tuesday 16th March – 18:30-22:30
Louth New Theatre, Main Square, Louth LL2 LLM

PERFORMANCES:
Wednesday 17th March-Saturday 20th March – 19:30
Louth New Theatre, Main Square, Louth LL2 LLM
Dress Code: Smart black clothing for all performances

I have attached a map showing how to get to the rehearsal venue and theatre. When you arrive at the theatre please sign in at Stage Door (on Chenworth Street) before making your way down to the orchestra pit. The all-inclusive fee of £400 will be paid by cheque after the final performance. Please provide an invoice for the full amount made out to "Louth Operatic Society". If there are any problems, or if anything needs clarifying, please feel free to call, otherwise I look forward to seeing you at the band call.

Yours sincerely,

Grace Morley (Musical Director)

Depending on the production company (and the budget) the responsibility for booking the band may be delegated to an Orchestral Manager/Orchestral Contractor, in which case it will be your responsibility as the Musical Director to liaise with the Orchestral Manager about the choice of musicians and any other issues such as rehearsal times, rehearsal venues and equipment/instrument hire and porterage.

Orchestral Manager/Contractor – (also referred to as the "fixer") The Orchestral Manager/Contractor is the person who is responsible for engaging and managing the musicians in the orchestra/band. They are often employed for larger/professional productions, and they normally work on a percentage fee agreement (ie: they charge the Production Company a percentage of the total musicians wages as their fee). They will be responsible for sorting wages, agreeing substitutes/deputies (in consultation with the Musical Director), dealing with disciplinary issues, liaising with the Musicians Union (MU) or the American Federation of Musicians (AFM), and also the general upkeep of the band. A good Orchestral Manager will ensure the musicians engaged are appropriate for the style of music being played, and will keep a close watch to ensure that a high musical standard is being maintained. Many successful Orchestral Managers are good musicians themselves, and often have personal experience of working in the professional music industry.

BAND/ORCHESTRA REHEARSALS

The Band/Orchestra rehearsals will normally take place near the end of the rehearsal process, often in the days leading up to the technical (tech.) rehearsals. These will either take place in a rehearsal room near to where the cast are rehearsing, in a separate rehearsal room, or sometimes in the theatre/performance space itself (the bar area being a common place – sadly with the bar closed!)

Contact List

It is useful to create a contact list containing all of the musicians' phone numbers. Ideally, you should also store their numbers in your mobile phone, and make sure your phone is turned on and fully charged in the hours leading up to the orchestra rehearsals. Ensure that all of the musicians have your phone number so that they can contact you if they require further clarification of any rehearsal/performance details, or if they get lost or delayed en-route to the rehearsal.

As with your vocal rehearsals, you should plan what you need to achieve in your band rehearsal(s). Remember that musicians have a different work ethic to actors. An actor will want to know *why* they are singing lyrics, what the context is, and will often be happy to discuss, in depth, the meaning of the lyrics. Musicians will be less keen to spend hours talking about the music, and prefer more time actually playing it. By all means, tell the musicians the context of the music they are playing if you feel it is relevant and will aid their performance, but avoid lecturing them on the subtext and in-depth feelings of the characters.

As mentioned earlier you should plan and practice exactly how you will conduct the show in advance of the band call. Take care to work out how you will conduct tricky passages and what your beat patterns and sub-divisions will be. This will save both you and the musicians precious time in the rehearsal room, and if you are clear about what you are doing, it will certainly be clearer for the musicians. Note that it is often easiest to conduct the music as it is written i.e. conduct music written in 4/4 in 4 (unless it feels very uncomfortable and unclear). You only need to tell the band if you are doing anything out-of-the-ordinary, or different to that which has been printed.

Highlight areas of technical difficulty, and let the players know about any tricky moments that you have to navigate (such as musical "hits" that are timed with specific stage movements, or passages of music that are timed with choreography/scene changes etc.).

Be very clear when marking cuts and changes and always mark these in using a pencil – never a pen. Things can often change, even in the later stages of the rehearsal process, and pen doesn't rub out very well! Explain cuts in a non-ambiguous way. For example: you could either say "cut bars 22-28" or "tacet from the start of bar 22 through to the end of bar 28". Both could mean the same thing, but the latter leaves no room for confusion.

If you are working with Musicians who are members of the Musicians Union (MU), American Federation of Musicians (AFM) or any other union body, or you are working on larger-scale semi-professional or professional productions, take time to read through the relevant union agreements so you are clear on when you need to give breaks, and also what the rules are concerning call times and lengths. (This also applies if you are working in a recording studio with union musicians). The MU and AFM are keen to protect musicians and their rights (which is, of course, a good thing for all musicians), so it is vital that the Musical Director is aware of these rules and regulations and can adhere to them. This also applies to Equity - the Actors union, and their own specific rules and regulations on working hours and rehearsal lengths.

The Sitzprobe and Wandelprobe

The **Sitzprobe** is the rehearsal where the Cast and Orchestra sing and play through the music for the whole show together, for the first time. Many will agree that this is one of the most exciting calls in any rehearsal process. The cast, who have often rehearsed with a simple piano accompaniment, get to hear the orchestrations for the first time; and the musicians get to hear what they are accompanying for the first time. As the Musical Director, this is very much your call, and can often be quite pressured, as you will have to deal with lots of excited and sometimes tired singers and musicians, who in the excitement may often forget to watch for cues, or forget to follow your conducting! You should tread a fine line between being overly firm and being in control - but take care not to get stressed and inadvertently kill the excitement. Make sure that you enjoy the experience, hearing it all come together for the first time, and also ensure that you use the rehearsal time wisely to cover all the important cues, taking time to clarify any difficult "corners" for everyone involved. Keep an eye on the clock and plan how long you have to rehearse each number. Consider the rehearsal time logically and only play a number more than once if you need to. As with your other rehearsals, make sure you start on time and don't tolerate bad time keeping from your musicians or actors.

The **Wandelprobe** is essentially the same as the Sitzprobe but with the cast doing some minor blocking/staging whilst they sing. This can be effective if rehearsal time is short and you want to maximize rehearsal time, but it can also lead to actors being distracted by staging issues and result in them paying less attention to the music (which is essentially the point of the rehearsal).

If possible you should arrange to use microphones and a small PA system for the Sitzprobe/Wandelprobe, otherwise there is a danger that the cast will over-sing (and potentially strain or damage their voices) in order to be heard over the musicians.

Musicians Union – Often referred to as the "MU". This is the British Union that look after all types of Musicians. They offer advice on contracts, suggested fees for performing and arranging work, and negotiate with Theatre Managing Bodies regarding pay, working conditions and anything else that may arise! For more information check out their website: www.musiciansunion.org.uk

American Federation of Musicians – also referred to as the "AFM". The American Union looking after the welfare of musicians. They are on hand to offer guidance and advice on negotiating fair agreements, protecting ownership of recorded music, securing benefits such as health care and pension. The AFM is the largest organization in the world representing the interests of professional musicians. For more information check out their website: www.afm.org

Chapter 6: **In the theatre**

Towards the end of the rehearsal period you will make the move from the rehearsal room into the theatre (unless you have been using the theatre/performance space as your rehearsal space). In amateur theatre, this move will normally happen on the Sunday or Monday of Performance Week (as the Theatre will normally be booked on a week hire period – Sunday morning-Saturday evening, with Sunday being the "get in" day for the technical team). In professional theatre, this move will normally happen just before you begin the technical rehearsals. This could be anytime from 3 or 4 days to several weeks prior to opening night, depending on the specific production.

Once you are in the theatre there are several key rehearsals that will take place before the first performance.

TECHNICAL REHEARSAL(S)
(OFTEN JUST REFERRED TO AS *"TECH."*)

The format for technical rehearsals varies greatly depending on the size and budget of the production. In amateur productions the "tech" rehearsal will often take place the day before the dress rehearsal (or "dress run") and will normally take the form of a stop-start full run of the show (usually accompanied by the full orchestra). This call will also serve as the "Stage & Orchestra" rehearsal (see page 135). A certain level of "dry–teching" (working through the technical cues without the cast) will hopefully have taken place before the Actors and Musicians arrive, and you will stop and start as required as you work your way through the show. In semi-professional and professional productions, the tech. rehearsal(s) will normally take place with piano accompaniment (although sometimes the Musical Director and Choreographer may decide to have a drummer present as well. This is common practice for shows that involve a lot of dance routines, as the beat is helpful for the dancers when they are running numbers, helping create a stronger sense of "time" than just a solo piano.)

Technical rehearsals for professional productions can vary greatly in length, depending on how "technical" the show is that you are working on. If the set is quite basic and there is relatively little flying of scenery or complex set movements, it may only take a few days. On larger shows where the set is more complex, possibly incorporating revolving stages, hydraulics, fast scenery changes, and complex lighting and effects, the tech. rehearsal may take several weeks.

The technical rehearsal is designed to sort out any *technical* aspects of the show, not about rehearsing the artistic elements (i.e.: acting, dancing and singing), so you should aim to have all of your work completed by the time you start to *tech.* the show.

SPECIFIC MUSIC AND SOUND REHEARSALS IN THE THEATRE

There are several specific music and sound rehearsals which occur once you have moved into the Theatre. These calls are:

- <u>Orchestra Seating Call</u> – where the musicians move into the orchestra pit/band area for the first time. This rehearsal is to make sure that everyone has enough room, and to check sight lines with the conductor (and each other, as appropriate).

  ☼ Make sure you check out the band pit prior to the band arriving, to make sure it has everything that they/you need. Make yourself a checklist to ensure you don't miss anything:

  - ☑ Music Stands (with lights)
  - ☑ Chairs for all the musicians
  - ☑ The orchestral/band music/parts (if the musicians didn't take them away)
  - ☑ Enough power points for any electric instruments*

*Always check with the sound team where to take your power for the electric instruments (guitars and keyboards) from, as they will often use a different electrical phase (different power source) for the sound and lighting equipment to help prevent any interference or mains hum.

- Sound Check – where you have time to check the stage fold-back (on-stage speaker system so the cast can hear the band) and the band fold-back (so the band can hear themselves in the band pit). This is also a time for the sound operator(s) to check the microphones and to perform any EQ work (adjusting the graphic equalization on each microphone/instrument channel so that it gives the optimum sound quality) required for the cast/band.

- Stage & Orchestra Rehearsal – This call gives the Musical Director stage time with the full cast (in microphones) and the full Orchestra/Band, to play through some musical numbers and check that everyone can hear everything they need in the fold-back and can clearly see the Conductor for all the cues. This call is also important for the sound department, as they will need time with the full cast and orchestra to set levels prior to the dress rehearsal(s).

THE ORCHESTRA PIT

The Orchestra Pit is a generic term used for describing the area where the musicians are set for the show. In some cases, this will be in a Pit, traditionally in-front of the stage and often sunk below the level of the audience seating (thus allowing the singers to sing *over* the musicians – quite literally). Normally the Conductor stands on a raised podium in the pit so that they can be seen by the musicians (looking up from the pit) and the cast (looking down from the stage).

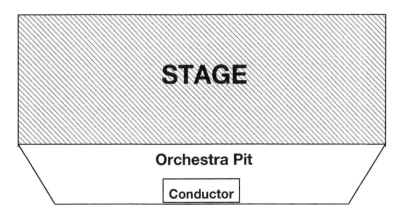

Whilst there are no hard and fast rules governing how the musicians are to be set out in the Orchestra Pit, a conventional orchestration (including *Rhythm Section, Strings, Woodwind, Brass* and *Drums/Percussion*) may be set out something like this:

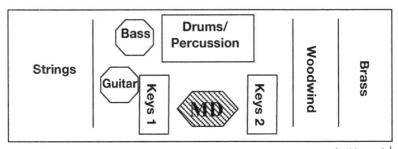

(not to scale)

As technology has advanced, and complex sound systems have been introduced to theatres and performance spaces, it has become possible to give the singers microphones so that they can be heard above the band (which nowadays, will often include amplified instruments such as keyboards and guitars). This has led to more advanced sound systems, and it is now common practice to place microphones on all the instruments (acoustic and electric) in the band/orchestra, so the sound operator has complete control over the mix of singers and the accompaniment. This means that the band can be situated almost anywhere in the theatre, sometimes in a different room altogether (this is referred to as the band being "remote"). When the band is "remote", the sound is relayed back to the auditorium through the main PA System (see page 138), and to the cast via on-stage monitoring/fold-back. A camera will normally be focussed on the Conductor, and TV monitors placed in the auditorium/performing space so the cast can see the Conductor for cues. (In larger theatres the Conductor monitors will often be placed on the front of the Dress Circle/Mezzanine.) This is common practice even if the Musical Director is conducting from the Orchestra Pit to avoid the cast constantly looking down for cues and thus breaking their eye line with the audience.

As sound and video relay equipment has dropped in price and has become more readily available, an increasing number of amateur and school/college shows are opting to have the band "remote", especially for Rock/Pop shows where balancing the sound in smaller halls, so the audience can hear the singers, can be difficult.

Here are some of the difficulties that may arise when working with a remote band:

- It can be difficult to lock in with the singers, as there isn't any personal connection as there would be if you were looking up at them from the Pit. It is therefore important that you teach the cast the musical cues in such a way that they are not reliant solely on visual cues (wherever possible). If you and the cast are consistent in rehearsals and performance this will make life easier once you are working "remotely".

- You are totally reliant on the monitoring system (visual and audio). Cueing has to be done by watching the *show relay* on a monitor, rather than seeing the stage in front of you. This can be difficult when you have to co-ordinate musical cues with a specific piece of staging or stage action (lighting or set). It is vitally important that you pay extra attention during the staging and technical rehearsals so that you are aware of what to look for.

Show Relay – A live video relay of the show that is used by Stage Management, the Musical Director and the Resident Director/Company Manager to see the show for cueing (Lighting, Sound and/or Music), and sometimes for noting (Actors, Dancers and/or Technical). The relay feed is normally taken from a fixed camera looking directly at the stage (often placed on the front of the Dress Circle/Mezzanine or an equivalent position). In most theatres there is normally an audio relay of the performance backstage (playing through fixed tannoy speakers in the corridors, dressing rooms and the Green Room so the cast and crew can hear what point they are at in the performance).

PA (Public Address) System – Sometimes referred to as a "Sound Reinforcement" (SR) System. These are general terms used to describe a system used to amplify the sound (speech or music) in a public place. It consists of an amplifier, sound source (live or recorded – in our case the Cast and Band are the sound source) and any number of speakers. In a large auditorium the PA system may use several banks of amplifiers and lots of different sized speakers carefully placed to deliver the sound to all the different seating areas. In smaller venues it may be a much simpler system with two speakers (one either side of the Stage) and one amplifier. Portable PA systems are also available in various sizes depending on your sound reinforcement requirements.

DESIGNING YOUR OWN ORCHESTRA PIT

There are no specific plans for how an Orchestra Pit should be laid out, so it would usually be the job of the Musical Director to plan where they would like everyone to be placed. Here are a few points to consider when planning your pit layout:

- If possible, try to keep the *Rhythm Section* (Piano, Bass, Drums and Guitar) together. The Bassist and Drummer in particular should be next to each other if at all possible, as they like to "lock in" with one another's playing, and will form the foundations for "the groove". It is also important that you are as close to the drummer and 1st keyboard player as possible, as these are normally the musicians who lead the orchestration. Ideally, you should position the drummer directly in front of you or just to the left of you (as you look down from your podium) – assuming they have their music stand just behind their hi-hats. This way, they will be able to see you in their peripheral vision as they are looking at their music.
- Try to keep each family of instruments together. For example: The flute/sax player next to the other woodwind players. This will ensure they can play as a section (as they would in an orchestra), and will help them in their phrasing and tuning. (This also applies to the Brass, Strings and Percussion.)

- Wherever possible, avoid placing the string players next to the drums/percussion, and avoid putting anybody's chair directly next to the crash cymbal as this may damage their hearing! It is best to place the *louder* instruments together (e.g.: the brass near the percussion and the woodwind near to the strings).
- If the Orchestra/Band is being amplified in any way ("miked" up), it is worth checking with the theatre staff to see if they have any Perspex screens or other sound absorbing screens, so you can close-off the drums/percussion and brass in the pit. This will help to make the pit acoustically quieter, and will also make life easier for the sound operator too as there will be less *spill* in the pit (different instruments "spilling" into individual microphones, e.g.: the flute microphone picking up the sound of the trumpet).
- Make sure everyone can see you. The Musicians need to have good sightlines with the Conductor, and with the other members of their section.
- Check that all the players have enough room to actually *play* their instruments. A trombonist will need room to use their slide, and string players will need room to bow. If in doubt, call them up and ask in advance.
- Make sure that everyone has access to their seats, and that the exits from the Pit are kept clear. Also, make sure you are complying with the Heath and Safety policy of the Theatre.

Next time you go to the Theatre, look in the Band/Orchestra Pit and see how it has been set out. Make a note of which instruments are sitting together (or near each other), and where the microphones and any sound absorbing/reflecting screens have been placed.

PIT RULES

It's the Musical Director's responsibility to maintain an orderly and professional working atmosphere in the pit. A few common "rules" are:

- No drinking of anything other than bottled water in the pit.
- Make sure drinks are never left near electrical equipment or power points (for obvious reasons!)
- Talking should be kept to an absolute minimum, as it can disturb the audience and will be picked up by any microphones in the pit.
- No food should ever be consumed in the pit. This is especially important in older theatres, as any traces of food can encourage mice and other rodents.

You should also take time to read the Health and Safety regulations relating to the band area, ensuring that all the musicians know where the fire exits are, and any other safety issues that are relevant to them.

SMILE - YOU'RE ON CAMERA!

As mentioned earlier it is common practice for a camera to be placed on the Conductor so that they can be seen by the cast, stage management (for cueing) and sometimes by members of the band (if it is difficult to achieve good sightlines within the Pit). Make sure that the camera is in a position that is comfortable for you to conduct into. Avoid the camera placement being too low, too high, or off to one side. Ideally, it will be placed centrally and at your conducting height.

Here are some other considerations when working on camera:

- The camera is on all of the time and you never know who is watching; therefore you should avoid yawning, playing around, picking your nose, or any other gestures that may be seen as rude or inappropriate.

- Make sure your *conducting box* (see Appendix – Conducting Technique) doesn't take your beat out of the camera view (i.e.: don't beat too high or too low, otherwise your beat will be lost on the screen).
- Don't be afraid to conduct directly *to* the camera (as if you were in front of the Cast). As you only appear two-dimensional on the screen (and often in black and white) you need to work even harder to keep the energy levels up.

THE DRESS REHEARSAL(S)

Depending on time you will have one, or perhaps two or three dress rehearsals. In the ideal world a dress rehearsal is a full run of the show (without stopping), as if it were a proper performance. The dress rehearsal will take place with a full cast (in costume), full orchestra and with full technical support (lights, sound, special FX and full set). Afterwards there will normally be time set aside for the Director, Choreographer and Musical Director to give notes to the cast. This will either be done separately (i.e.: all acting notes, followed by all dance notes, followed by all musical notes), or in chronological show order (i.e.: each department gives notes on each song or scene in turn, then moves on to the next song/scene). A meeting between the Artistic Team and the Technical Team (either formal or informal) will normally follow directly after the cast have been broken (after their "notes" session), to discuss the dress rehearsal and resolve any issues that may have arisen.

PREPARING TO CONDUCT A PERFORMANCE

Before conducting a performance, it is important that you prepare yourself mentally and physically for the task ahead. Aim to get down to the Pit before "beginners" (the call 5 minutes before the curtain goes up) so you can greet the musicians, check that you have the substitutes/deputies you were expecting (if any), check that your score is set up as you want it, and generally get yourself "in the zone" ready to conduct the show. When you are conducting you are also performing yourself - as well as leading others in performance. The musical inspiration for the actors and musicians stems from you, so it is vital that you look *and feel* ready to give a performance to the best of your ability when the curtain rises on your show.

When the *cue light* goes green, and the house lights dim you have a responsibility to all the people on both sides of the *Proscenium Arch* to deliver the goods, so it is vital that you always commit to the performance 100% and give it your all.

> **"Proscenium Arch" Theatre** - a theatre space whose characteristic feature is a large archway (the proscenium arch) at or near the front of the stage. The audience faces the stage, which is normally raised several feet above the front row of the audience. There are often curtains that are either drawn across, or are flown in, to cover the archway and thus mask the stage area from the audience. The area in front of the curtain is called the apron. The areas obscured by the proscenium arch are called the wings, and there are normally curtains to mask the wings so that the audience cannot see offstage. Proscenium stages vary greatly in size and can range from one to several stories high.

Back stage calls (announcements) are made through a tannoy system, which is a speaker relay system heard only backstage, in corridors and dressing rooms. There are several standard backstage calls that you will normally hear before the show. These are:

- "The Half" – 35 minutes before the curtain rises. As a rule, all the cast have to be signed into the building by the half.
- "The Quarter" – 20 minutes before the curtain rises. Normally the "quarter hour call" will announce which covers are on for that performance, and who will be conducting.
- "The five" – 10 minutes before the curtain rises.
- "Beginners" – 5 minutes before the curtain rises, when all of the ACT 1 (or 2) "beginners" are called to the stage (i.e.: anyone who is on-stage for the opening of the show). The "Musical Director and Ladies and Gentlemen of the Orchestra" will also be called to the stage/pit during this call.

GIVING NOTES ON PERFORMANCES

Part of your duties as the Musical Director is to give notes to the actors and musicians when necessary to do so. It is important when you are conducting a run of a show (i.e. a show that runs for more than one performance) that you maintain the standard that you initially set in the rehearsal room. Over time some of the finer details that you have worked on will fade and be forgotten so it is vital that you keep an ear open for anything you cannot hear which should be there, and also for anything which has crept in and is unwelcome, such as inappropriate phrasing, riffing or subtle changes to the melody, changes to vibrato and other voice/tonal qualities that you set in rehearsals, over or under singing and breath points.

When giving notes you must keep in mind that people who work in "The Arts" (especially performing arts, such as singers, dancers, actors and musicians) are often more sensitive than people who work in a "nine 'til five" job. The lifestyle of a performer can be an emotional rollercoaster, and this is often reflected in the performer's personalities.

Always think about the best way to give a note and what you want to achieve by giving it. A note will normally be given either after a performance or before the next performance (often after the vocal warm-up). You should avoid giving notes mid way through a show as you run the risk of distracting the actor from the rest of their performance.

There are often two ways in which you can say the same thing. For example, if a singer is flat on a certain note you could say: "you're flat at bar 21, sing it in tune next time" or you could say "just take a bit of care over that note in bar 21. It's a bit under, so try lifting it up a bit (or brightening the tone etc...)". Both notes convey the same meaning, but the latter is less likely to upset the performer. In reality, if you upset someone by giving notes in a brutal way this may make them paranoid and nervous, which may lead to them giving a worse performance next time.

- Think about ways to give notes to specific performers. Consider the individual and what to say to get the best out of them.
- There is a proper time and place to exert your musical authority, and sometimes you will need to be firm with singers/actors and musicians to achieve the musical results that you require.
- If you feel that notes aren't being taken on board, call a rehearsal so you can fix the problem.
- If you ever have issues with a performer not responding to your notes, or not treating you with professional respect, you may need to adopt a more stern approach. If problems persist you should make your concerns known to the [Resident] Director and Company Manager, and ask for their advice, assistance or support. If you have a Musical Supervisor you can also seek their advice and guidance. Remember to listen to every viewpoint, and always act with respect and dignity. Equally, if members of the cast or any of the musicians come to you for help and advice, always take time to listen to them and offer any help that you can. I'm sure most experienced Musical Directors would agree that Musical Direction often feels like 80% people management and 20% music (especially on longer running productions).
- Keep a note pad on your stand so you can make notes on the Cast and Orchestra during a performance.
- It is common practice (and professional courtesy) to give notes to principal actors privately in their/your dressing room, as opposed to in front of the full company.

TROUBLESHOOTING

Here are some problems you may encounter either during rehearsals or in performances, and a possible solution:

- **The Cast are singing out of tune** – Can they hear themselves properly, and can they hear the piano (or instrument they are tuning to)? Is the fold-back too quiet or too loud and overpowering?

Solution – Ask the sound operator to adjust the fold-back (or position a separate speaker on/near the stage) so the cast can hear what they need to tune to. If it is too loud, they will over-sing and push it sharp (and may lose their voices as a result of forcing the tone). You should avoid having the fold-back (and the main PA system) too loud for these reasons.

- **The Cast/Band are not following your beat** – Can they see you properly? Are they being distracted by lots of other things happening around them?
  Solution – If they can't see you because it's too dark, ask the Technical Team if they can position a narrow spotlight on you so everyone can see your beat (a "special"). If you feel that the actors or musicians are being distracted, ask them to focus on you, reminding them which specific cues they must watch you for, and really try to make your beat sharp and clear. In other words, make sure you are giving them something worth watching!

- **The Cast are losing their harmonies** – Perhaps they need reminding where to find their starting notes (in relation to the vocal or instrumental line before they sing).
  Solution - If they are used to hearing a cue on a piano and it is now played within the Orchestra, they may need telling where to listen out for it (e.g. on the oboe, etc....) If they are still struggling then perhaps try relating their first notes to the line before, perhaps using the "famous songs" intervals from Chapter 2.

- **The Cast are not singing together** – Do the cast sound messy and unfocussed?
  Solution – Remind the cast to focus on their own ensemble work and point out a few specific moments that require attention. Also remind them to listen to one another and concentrate on blending their sound into the ensemble mix. Hopefully this note will help them focus generally, as well as during the specific moments you have highlighted.

CONDUCTING A RUN

Here are some thoughts on conducting a run of a show (i.e.: any number of consecutive performances):

- Make sure your tempos are consistent. Remember that fatigue, too much caffeine and being excited or stressed can affect your judgment. Take care to regularly check your tempos with a metronome, and make sure you are giving a consistent performance. Over a long run the fast numbers will often get faster (supposedly to keep the "energy" up), and the slow numbers will get slower as people start to indulge in them. Keep an eye on this and avoid falling into these common tempo traps.
- Take care that your cueing is the same from show to show as the Actors, Musicians and stage crew will get used to the way you are giving cues, entries and bring offs, and any deviation from what they are expecting may throw them.
- If you plan to change anything (cues, orchestration, tempos, etc.), make sure you tell the Actors, Musicians and Stage Management/Sound Team <u>before</u> the performance.
- Record the show from time to time (ideally from a Front of House position so you are hearing it as the audience does) and take time to listen to the recording, so you can note yourself and the cast.
- When conducting a long run, try to get out to watch the show during a performance (by asking your assistant/cover conductor to conduct the show). Listen to the mix from the sound desk and note the performance (band, cast and whoever is conducting in your place). You can also chat to the sound engineer about the mix and share any thoughts that you have with them, which may help to further enhance the sound of the show.
- Never let the size of the audience affect the performance. It is easy when the curtain goes up to reveal a small house to let the energy drop on-stage and in the Pit. **You must work against this**. The audience members (however few) have paid to watch a show, so you must make sure you give them their money's worth.

THEATRICAL SUPERSTITIONS

You may well have already heard that it is bad luck to wish a performer "good luck" on opening night (and indeed, there is a song about just that in "The Producers"). Instead, you should say "break a leg" which is the theatrical equivalent of saying "good luck". This doesn't literally mean "go on and break your leg!" but originates from the time of King James I, when the audience would throw coins on-stage during the curtain calls/bows to "tip" the actors (as a means of expressing their enjoyment of the performance.) The actors would then kneel down to collect the coins from the floor, hence breaking their leg line as they knelt. However, if they didn't enjoy the performance they would often throw rotten fruit at the performers instead! These traditions have disappeared from modern day theatre and have now developed into throwing flowers on stage during the curtain calls/bows, or presenting bouquets to the leading actors as a sign of your appreciation for the performance. The way to show your disapproval of a particular performer or performance nowadays is to write a disparaging review on-line or in a newspaper. Throwing rotten fruit at the performers nowadays will probably get you thrown out of the theatre!

It is also considered bad luck to mention "Macbeth" in a theatre as it is thought to bring bad luck to the production. Two reasons lie behind this myth. Firstly because there are numerous documented mishaps surrounding performances of "Macbeth", including accidents, illness and even deaths; and secondly, because in the past, struggling theatre companies have mounted a production of "Macbeth" at the end of a difficult season in order to pull in an audience and make the season break-even financially. However, even this popular play has sometimes not raised enough income at the box office to save the struggling company, and they have been forced to close at the end of the season anyway. This has resulted in "Macbeth" becoming associated with bad business and the entire company being made redundant. It is therefore considered very bad luck to mention "Macbeth" in any theatre, and you should instead refer to it as "The Scottish Play". What curious people theatre folk are!

MD Wardrobe (Male)

Evening Dress/DJ:
Black Dinner Suit
White Shirt
Black Bow Tie
Smart Shoes

Smart Blacks:
Black Suit (maybe)
Smart Black Shirt
Black Trousers
Black Shoes

Casual Blacks:
Plain black shirt/
tee shirt
Black trousers/Jeans
Plain black casual
shoes/trainers/boots

MD Wardrobe (Female)

Evening Dress:
Smart, formal black
dress/suit
Black shoes

Smart Blacks:
Smart black top/blouse
Smart skirt/trousers
Smart black
shoes/boots

Casual Blacks:
Plain black top
Black trousers/jeans
Plain black casual
shoes/trainers/boots

Chapter 7:
The Tailor Made Musical Director

The Musical Director's roles and responsibilities vary from job to job, so it is important that you tailor your work so that it fits the remit of the project that you are working on.

TAILORING YOUR REHEARSAL TECHNIQUE FOR THE GROUP YOU ARE WORKING WITH

Every Musical Director has their own way of rehearsing a company, and they will develop their own individual style and rehearsal manner over time. Whatever your rehearsal method, you should always keep in mind the ultimate goal of teaching the score to the best of everyone's ability, and ensuring that this is achieved in the allocated rehearsal time.

As you gain experience participating in, assisting and leading rehearsals, you will invariably find your own method of working. Here are a few thoughts to consider when working with specific age ranges:

- **Working with Children** When working with children it is important that you strive to keep the energy level up. Younger children (11 years and below) will find it hard to concentrate through long vocal rehearsals, so try to work in short sessions wherever possible (50mins or less is ideal). Take the time to explain things clearly, but avoid long and deep discussions about the lyrics, as this may go over most of their heads. Remember that the children you are working with will have limited life experience (compared to you), so avoid referring to things that they won't, as yet, have any understanding of. Using *imagery* can work well; for example, you might ask them to sing with the feeling of walking into a sweet shop and being able to eat as many sweets as they like *or* the feeling when they get an A+ for their homework. Playing competitive games can also be very effective, such as dividing the room in half and seeing which side can sing the loudest or softest, most beautiful/dreamy, the happiest or saddest. Take care not to speak down to, or patronize the group as this will invariably have a negative effect. You should endeavour to strike a fine line between being firm, but also energized, lively and enthusiastic.

- **Working with Teenagers** – Like working with children it is vital that you don't speak down to teenagers. If you know your stuff and are confident in the way you teach they will ultimately grow to respect you. Avoid being old fashioned or playing the "old school teacher" card. Remember that you cannot *command* respect - you can only *earn* it. Equally, if you give them an inch – they'll take a mile, so don't be afraid to run a tight ship. As long as your work method (however strict) achieves good results, this is the main thing. The moment the group feels that they are getting good results and vocally "gelling", they will respect you for that. If you go in too soft, and try to be "one of them" and their friend, it will be hard to pull it back if you ever need to - so always try to maintain the respect barrier. Often with teenagers, the higher the goals you set the better they will be, so never be afraid to challenge them mentally and vocally.

- **Working with Adults** – If you are a younger Musical Director who is just starting out, you may find yourself rehearsing an adult Amateur Dramatic/Community Theatre Company where some of the members are possibly double your age! Or, if you are a recent college graduate preparing to conduct a drama school/college production, you may find that you are teaching people older than yourself. Remember that in every situation you must respect the performers who you are working with – both musically, and (in these specific instances) for their *greater* life experience. Nobody likes being spoken down to in a rehearsal room, and this is amplified further if it is by someone considerably younger than themselves. Try to make the rehearsals enjoyable and work at a speed that the group can cope with. Avoid playing copious musical games (as you perhaps would with younger people), and don't drive them so hard that you lose focus. Take care not to be patronizing in your rehearsal manner, and try to put your musical stamp on the production without walking all over people and being disrespectful, as this will only lead to mutiny in the ranks!

CONDUCTING A SHOW CHOIR

Since the American TV show "Glee" hit the screens in 2009 interest in *Show Choirs* has grown considerably, not only in America but also in the UK. This primarily American art form involves a close bond between singing and dance, and it is therefore vital that the Musical Director has a good working relationship with the Choreographer. As well as mutual respect for one another's disciplines, it is important that you appreciate the demands of singing and dancing on the performers themselves. You must take care that your demands are within the achievable goals of the group that you are working with. Of course, it's important to stretch everyone to their maximum potential, but if you stretch things too far they tend to break! As we mentioned earlier it requires great physical stamina to sing and dance at the same time, and you should consider this when planning the routines (both musical and choreographic).

When you are preparing for a Competition or Invitational you will need to work closely with the Choreographer and Choir Director to ensure that the music requirements marry with the dance requirements, and that it all falls within the rules and guidelines of the competition. You will also need to make sure that the arrangements are all written to the specifications which you require (i.e. the size of your band/combo and the keys and structures you have decided upon), or if you are using hired/bought arrangements, that these fit musically with what you have taught, and that you check them through with the choreographer, making sure that there are no surprises at the first band call!

- When you are rehearsing, try to maintain a positive "can-do" attitude. Negativity can only bring the mood of the group down.
- Keep your rehearsals crisp and snappy. Enjoyable and energized rehearsals will make people want to attend

every practice, which is vital for the success of the Show Choir.

- Encourage good posture, positive body language, raised eyebrows, warm smiles, and good facial expressions throughout.
- Encourage people to practice outside of rehearsals. Together with the Choir Director and Choreographer, offer to provide recordings of the music so that individuals can practice in their own time.

WORKING WITH NON-READING MUSICIANS

If you are working on a rock/pop project, be it a concert or a show you may find yourself working with musicians who don't read music, or who's music reading is comparatively basic. Lots of guitarists, bassists and drummers with a background in rock/pop initially learn to play by ear, practising along to recordings, and working from chord charts, as opposed to working from printed sheet music. This means their aural skills are often much more developed than their music reading skills. Never make the assumption that non-reading musicians are in any way lesser musicians. Many of the world's finest rock players are not confident music readers, despite being fantastic musicians.

If you are working on a rock musical (like "Jesus Christ Superstar", "The Rocky Horror Show" or "Hair"), you may find some of the musicians in your band come from a non-reading background and will therefore learn the show primarily by listening to, and playing along to recordings. It is therefore advisable to send them a reference recording of the show as you plan to do it. This may be a copy of one particular cast recording, or perhaps a compilation of various different recordings. Take care that the musicians are aware in advance of any changes of key or format, and if possible cut or edit a recording (this is relatively easy to do using "Logic" and other music recording/editing software), for the musicians to practise and refer to.

CONDUCTING A TOURING SHOW

If you find yourself engaged as the Musical Director for a professional touring production (either a *Book Musical* or a compilation show), take the time to read the union rules about touring (the MU and the AFM have a strict agreement in place to help protect musicians against unfair treatment). As the Musical Director, you are effectively head of the music department "on the road" (as the Music Supervisor will not normally tour with the show, and is just likely to visit from time to time). It is therefore your responsibility to make sure that both the management and the musicians are adhering to the rules and regulations, and to take action with the appropriate party if rules are broken.

- Make sure that the rules on minimum pay, as set out by the MU/AFM, are being observed and implicated.
- If a musician is doubling or trebling (i.e. playing more than one instrument), they will be due an additional payment (normally a percentage of their basic fee).
- If a performance begins after 11pm, or runs beyond midnight, additional payments are normally due. Check the relevant agreements, or call up the MU/AFM to ask their advice on this.
- Overtime and sick pay are payable, depending on the length of the contract. These rules vary between the UK/US, so seek the advice of the relevant union if necessary.
- Note that no performances are allowed to be recorded, unless the acting company and the musicians agree to it in advance. Normally the management (if they have been granted permission) can record up to three minutes of the show/performance to use for publicity and marketing. Make sure that no one (including members of the cast and band) are making recordings of the show without your knowledge.
- When you are on tour, you will be due a touring allowance/per diem and travel expenses.

WORKING WITH BACKING TRACKS

There are occasions when it won't be practical, or indeed possible to work with a live band. Sometimes this will be because the venue cannot accommodate live musicians due to space or volume/acoustic constraints; at other times it will be because the budget cannot permit the costs of engaging musicians and sourcing or commissioning the arrangements. On these occasions you and/or the creative team may decide to use backing tracks for the performances.

If you find yourself working with backing tracks, try to get hold of them as early as possible, especially if the music is particularly *rubato* or contains any *colla voce* passages. If this is the case, it is important for the artist to get used to the tracks so that they are confident when performing with them on stage.

When you are given the backing tracks (or after you have sourced them yourself), check that the song structure matches the sheet music which you are using in rehearsals, and that the harmonies tie-up with those in the score. Sometimes, for no apparent reason, backing tracks will contain subtle oddities (an extra bar, an additional chorus or bridge passage, or a change to the harmonisation of a particular passage of music), which can throw both you and the performer further down the line, if they are un-detected. It is therefore important that you check the tracks thoroughly before rehearsing with them.

MDING PANTOMIMES

Welcome to the wonderful world of Pantomime – a world where the romantic male lead is played by a woman, the Pantomime Dame is played by a man, the audience sing along and join in whenever they get the urge, and where two people stroll around the stage together dressed in a large "Daisy the cow" costume! Pantomimes are musical-comedy theatre productions, especially popular in the UK, Australia and Canada, and normally performed in the Winter months. (Frankly, you'll be hard pushed to find a Theatre or Church/Community Hall in England that *isn't* showing a Pantomime in December and January!)

For those who are new to the mad-cap world of Pantomime (often abbreviated to "Panto"), here are a few thoughts to help you along your way.

AUDIENCE PARTICIPATION

Contrary to traditional performance etiquette, it is expected that a Pantomime audience will be anything other than quiet throughout the performance. There are numerous traditions that can throw the unsuspecting performer (and Musical Director) if they are not familiar with this particular theatrical tradition.

- The audience will be encouraged to sing along to anything they know, and to call out to the cast on-stage whenever they get the urge. The Pantomime Dame will often interact with the audience, asking them to help her out if she gets stuck ("It's behind you" is a common call-out when people are sneaking up on one another). Audiences will also "boo" the *Baddies*, "cheer" the *Goodies* and "Aw" anything sweet or sentimental.
- During the time between the last scenes and the finale (where there is normally a Wedding or another kind of "happy ever after" ending), there will traditionally be a "song-sheet" number (led by the Dame and comedic side-kick) ,where the audience will sing along with the chorus – it is common practise to divide the audience in half to see which side can sing the loudest. The winning side will receive a prize – often some sweets thrown out into that side of the audience.

  If it falls to you to choose the "Song Sheet" song(s), pick something that has a catchy chorus, ideally something that is well known and/or current. A good example of a Song Sheet number is "Is this the way to Amarillo?", as the chorus is easily picked up, it's a simple lyric, and most people are familiar with the tune.

PICKING UP THE CUES

When you first read though the *Panto* script, make sure you have a pencil to hand to make a note of any musical cues which are either marked-in, or you think need adding. In Pantomimes it is expected of the Musical Director and the band to mark (pick up) any possible cue with a musical hit or "sting".

For example, a stage direction such as:

[THE DAME TRIPS OVER THE BASKET AND FALLS DOWN FLAT ON HER BOTTOM!]

..... is calling out for a Tom-Tom drag from your drummer. Make a note of this at the end of the line in your script.

- If anybody throws something across the stage, this should be marked with a *Siren Whistle*.
- When the flower wilts (Pantomimes are traditionally full of comedy props and costumes) this should be marked with a *Swanny Whistle* going down.
- When the fairy waves her magic wand, an ascending whole-tone scale played high up on bell-type keyboard sound marks the moment perfectly.

A Pantomime band will sometimes be quite small, sometimes even just a Musical Director/Pianist and Drummer. Because of the massive number of cues (especially percussion cues), it is often helpful to give all of the band (or at least the drummer) copies of the script and let them manage some of their own cues. Knowing the difficulties often associated with cueing trips, falls and throws, if the drummer has clear sightlines with the stage, it may be easier to let them cue themselves.

- If any of the musicians are taking cues directly from the stage, you will need to make sure their sightlines are good with both the stage and the conductor.
- Because of the numerous percussion cues/hits, it is common practice for several (sometimes all) of the members of the band to have percussion instruments to play to ensuring that all the cues can be covered, and to spread the stress!

THE PANTO SCORE.... OR LACK OF IT!

When you are working on a conventional *book* musical you will normally have a fully written-out vocal score and scripted storyline. Pantomimes, on the other hand, are often done with a make-shift score, traditionally comprising well-known songs (old and new) picked by the Director, Choreographer and Musical Director*. The song list will often include recent commercial music hits, re-worked traditional/folk songs, along with some Musical Theatre favourites. The lyrics are often *altered* or sometimes fully re-written so they fit in with the scene (sometimes rather tenuously), and the Musical Director will sometimes be given the task of re-arranging some of the songs to give them a different feel (either "updating" the original orchestration or changing the feel altogether – e.g. Frank Sinatra's "My Way" as a Rumba, or a hip-hop version of "Tomorrow" from Annie. There will sometimes be suggestions or guidelines in the script for the type of song the writer intended (e.g.: *Prince & Princess sing a love duet, affirming their love for one another and ending with a big kiss*).

---

* Note that some Pantomimes have commissioned scores with original songs, and would therefore be rehearsed like a conventional book show.

It is often part of the Musical Director's job to suggest songs to the Director and Choreographer (after reading the script), source the sheet music (or write it out as appropriate), prepare scores or lead sheets for the band, and to transpose songs as required (bearing in mind the romantic male role is traditionally played by a girl and the Pantomime Dame is traditionally played by a man – so songs written specifically for men and women will invariably need the keys altering to suit your specific Artistes.)

PREPARING YOUR PIANO/CONDUCTOR PAD

- Before you start rehearsals, make copies of all the music for yourself, so you can mark in any notes and pencil in cuts and changes.
- If the Choreographer or Director have asked for any music to be cut/made shorter try to work this out in advance and hence save valuable rehearsal time.
- Make notes of where you think there may need to be a play-off or scene change music in your script, and start to think about which music you might use.
- Ask the Director about the "Overture", "Entr'acte" and "Bows Music" and note down any ideas that you both have.
- Once the music is finalised, make a list of the Musical Numbers and prepare a list for yourself and the band. Reprises and scene changes can be written using numbers and letters. E.g. a reprise of song 5) can be labelled 5a) and the following scene change could be called 5b).

A DIFFERENT GIG EVERY SHOW!

Because there is an enormous amount of freedom in the world of Pantomime, and because the actors are often allowed to "play the crowd" and improvise around the script as they see fit, you should make sure you stay 100% alert at all times, ready to jump in from a different cue line, or with a musical accent/sting should the need arise (for example: a new joke is *ad libbed* in response to an audience shout and you feel the need to put a musical "button" on it, assuming the Director has allowed this kind of artistic license.)

A typical Panto musical "button":

A WORLD OF MUSICAL CLICHÉS

The unwritten rule in Pantomime is that pretty much anything goes! If you can "mark" a moment musically then you should. For this reason, all Panto Musical Directors should equip themselves with a dictionary of musical clichés.

For example, when the "Baddie" (the sinister character) enters you should give them some kind of entrance music (a short musical "sting" as they are often called). This can either be the standard:

...or perhaps something specifically associated with nasty characters, such as "Darth Vader's Theme" from "Star Wars".

Equally, when the Fairy God Mother waves her wand a magical tinkle from a mark tree, perhaps accompanied by an ascending whole-tone scale would help to mark the moment. A Brass Fanfare for the King as he enters, and a "clip-clop" on the temple-blocks (or coconut shells) as the Prince rides his *hobby-horse* to save the Princess are all ways in which the Musical Director and band can accentuate the action on-stage musically.

There are thousands of musical clichés to be found, but here are a few suggestions to start you off:

Chase Music:

Fanfare (for the Entrance of Royalty):

Ghost/"Creeping Around" Music:

Romantic Music:

"Baddie" Music:

Here are some further examples of famous musical clichés to add to your Panto tool-box:

- *Hearts & Flowers*   for "Sad" moments
- *James Bond Theme*   for Detective/Police scenarios
- *Mission Impossible*   for going on a mission/adventure
- *Superman Theme*   for Heroic moments
- *E.T. Flying Theme*   for Uplifting/Victorious moments
- *Brahms Lullaby/*   for Sleeping/child-like moments
  When you wish upon a star
- *Phantom of the Opera* for scary/"Baddie" music
- *"Morning" Peer Gynt*   to signify a new day/waking up
- *Ride of the Valkyries*   to signify riding into battle
- *O Fortuna*   for evil/big, scary moments
- *Chariots of Fire*   for slow motion/running moments

If a famous piece of music has been used as part of a television advert, a musical association can often be made to an emotion or mood. These can be referenced to provide good comic moments in Panto as well. An example of this is "Air on a G-String" used in the UK *Hamlet* Cigar adverts a few years ago. You could use this musical quote for a moment of pondering or reflection.

In the wonderful world of Pantomime there is a lot more musical freedom than there would be in a traditional book musical. The main thing is to enter the rehearsal process with an open mind, and treat the music as a melting pot that everyone can throw ideas into. There often isn't the time to be precious about the music (Pantomime rehearsal periods are often quite short – sometimes just one week for Professional Pantomime), so be open and receptive to ideas from your colleagues and, as with all Musical Directing jobs, always do what is best for the show *as a whole,* even if it is not always your personal musical ideal!

PANTOMIMES - A traditional British entertainment, generally performed around Christmas time. Pantomimes are also popular in Australia, Canada, Jamaica, South Africa, Japan, Ireland, Gibraltar and Malta. Pantomimes (or "Panto's") are light-hearted shows aimed at the whole family, written with a slap-stick style humour. The jokes are traditionally topical and satirical, and often the music will comprise or re-worked popular music that is adapted for the story. Pantomimes are most commonly based on traditional stories and fairy tales such as "Snow White and the Seven Dwarfs", "Sleeping Beauty", "Cinderella" etc..

See for yourself

If you've never seen a Pantomime and there is one playing at a theatre near you next Winter, make sure you go and check one out. They are a unique form of theatre – well worth a watch!

Chapter 8:
A note for aspiring professionals

If you aspire to be a full-time professional Musical Director I would strongly advise you to take on as many different and diverse jobs as possible – basically, do anything and everything you possibly can! This is especially important in the early stages of your career, as there is no substitute for experience. Unlike other performers (actors and instrumentalists), Musical Directors don't tend to audition for jobs - they either get a call asking them to come in for an informal chat/interview, or just a straight call offering them the gig. This means you have to get yourself known in the industry, so people know you are out there ready to work for them.

- **Build up your CV/Resume as much as possible**. Try to play in as many different venues as you can, and try to get your finger in as many pies as possible!
- **Keep yourself open to as many styles as possible.** Avoid being pigeon-holed as a musically *straight* conductor (someone who doesn't have the *feel or groove* to do rock/pop Musicals), or as a Pop/Rock conductor (someone who can only play grooves, with no sense of classical styles).
- **Do anything and everything.** If it fits in the diary then do it! Get yourself known as widely as possible. You never know who is watching you, or who they know – and who they might recommend you to, if they're impressed with your work.
- **Remember that you are only as good as your last gig.** Make sure everything that you work on is to your highest standard. **Never** "tier" your work - don't ever think "Oh, this is just a little Sunday gig so I'll *blag* this one". You never know who is watching and listening. Remember that bad news tends to travel even faster than good news, so never give anyone reason to criticise you and/or your work.

- **Learn from the people around you.** Always work with an open mind, and try to learn from *other people's* experiences. When you are working with people who have been in "the business" for a long time, observe how they work and see if you can pick up any "tried and tested" tips. Ask questions (at the appropriate time) and makes notes – mental and written – that you can refer back to at a later date.
- **Keep an eye out for new work opportunities.** Always check the main theatrical publications, such as "The Stage" (UK), "Casting Call Pro" (UK - online), "Backstage" (US) and "American Theatre" (US) for potential Musical Director jobs and don't be afraid to write to people to let them know you're ready, willing and able to work!
- **Keep your CV/Resume up to date.** Take the time to type-set your CV, always making sure you keep it current. The theatrical world can be quite "last-minute", so it's always good to have a CV ready should you require one.

Keeping your finger on the pulse

Always keep an eye on who's who in the professional theatre world. Read the programme/playbill thoroughly when you go to see a Show. Find out who the Musical Supervisor is, who the key Orchestral Contractors/Fixers are, who the rehearsal pianists were, who did the Orchestrations, and who's playing in the Band. The old saying "It's not what you know, it's who you know" is very true, especially in the theatre industry, so it's wise to keep your finger on the pulse.

In Conclusion

The art of Musical Direction involves lots of different musical and non-musical elements; from the technique of conducting an ensemble of Actors and Musicians through a performance, to diplomatic people management. Many of these elements have been discussed in this handbook, and hopefully it has given you an insight into how you can further develop the knowledge and skills required to musically direct a show.

The inspiration, passion and drive will come from the buzz you feel when you successfully conduct a performance, and the elation you feel when the cast and orchestra beam from cheek to cheek during the final curtain calls. In the words of Irving Berlin – "There's no business like show business"!

Stuart Morley
December, 2011

Appendix 1:
Conducting Technique

BEAT PATTERNS

For those readers wishing to learn the conducting beat patterns, or who are looking for a refresher, please study the beat patterns overleaf. They should be so ingrained that they are instinctive, such that you don't need to think about them whilst conducting a performance.

- Conducting style is highly personal. As long as it is clear and easy to follow, there are very few hard-and-fast rules, so have a go, and see what works best for you.

- Beat 1 always goes straight down, and the final beat (the "up-beat") always goes up (from the outside-in).

- The beat should start from the same imaginary plane that it lands on. The eye can perceive this plane and hence predict at what point the beat will land back there. This is how we know where the beat is (sometimes called the "beat line").

- The beat should never stop moving. Make sure there are no "kinks" in your beat when you practice. Always think in curves.

4 beats in a bar:

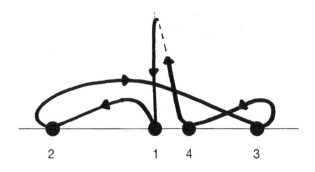

3 beats in a bar:

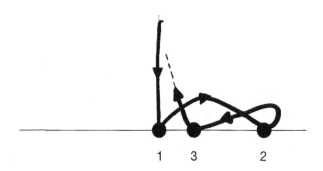

2 beats in a bar:

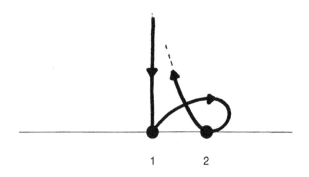

1 beat in a bar:

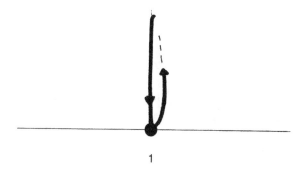

1

5 beats in a bar (2+3):

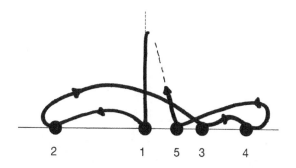

2   1 5 3   4

5 beats in a bar (3+2):

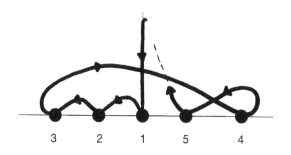

3   2   1   5   4

6 beats in a bar:

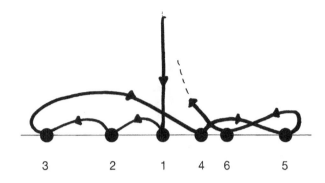

To beat 8, 9 10 and beyond, you simply add an extra smaller bounce at each beat point. Here's an example of an 8 beat pattern (subdivided 4):

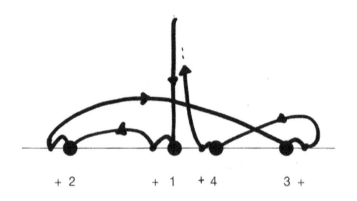

GET PRACTICING

- Practice sub-dividing all the beat patterns, starting the sub-division on any beat of the bar.

- Learn all beat patterns with both hands. This is not because you should mirror your beat in both hands, in fact this should be avoided as it is un-necessary and distracting; but because there may be times when you are conducting (especially from the keyboard), and will need to conduct and give cues with either hand. For this reason, you should aim to be an ambidextrous conductor.

Once you feel confident conducting all the different beat patterns you should practice alternating between them. You will often be required to change time signature whilst conducting, so it is useful to spend some time practicing this.

WHICH BEAT PATTERN SHOULD I USE?

Generally, you should use the beat pattern that *feels* right for the tempo you are conducting. For example, if a piece of music is written in a very fast 4/4, it may well feel easier to conduct it in 2. If a piece of music is in a slow 6/8, you may find it feels better to conduct it in 6. If it is a faster 6/8 it is common practice to conduct it in 2. When conducting complex time signatures, such as 5/8 or 7/8 at a faster tempo you should conduct the *group* breakdown instead of frantically trying to beat each individual beat. For example, if a bar of 7/8 is grouped as 3+2+2 (quavers), you would conduct an un-even 3-beat pattern - with the first beat lasting 3 quavers, and beats 2 and 3 lasting 2 quavers. For a bar of 5/8, grouped as a 2+3 you would conduct an un-even 2-beat pattern with the 1st beat lasting for 2 quavers and the 2nd beat lasting for 3 quavers.

Have a look at the following exercise, and spend time thinking about the mechanics of conducting it.

Before conducting through the exercise, try to familiarise yourself with the melody by either singing or playing it (or both). It is always easier to conduct a passage of music (especially if it is a tricky passage) if you are familiar with the melody.

Further Study

If you need to practice changing between the beat patterns have a look at: "The Worst Pies in London" from Sweeney Todd (Stephen Sondheim ✎ ♫). Study the score thoroughly, then try conducting along to several different recordings. This particular example is good for changing time signature whilst phrasing with the singer through fluid tempo changes.

Once you have mastered this, have a look at "Press Conference" from Chess (Tim Rice ✎ / Benny Andersson & Bjorn Ulvaeus ♫). This is another good exercise in changing time signature, here with a more constant tempo.

THE UP-BEAT

The most important beat is undoubtedly the up-beat. This is the beat that is given to indicate the start of the music, and from it the musicians have to gauge the tempo of the proceeding passage of music and determine the exact point at which you want them to play the first beat.

You should think of the up-beat as a preparatory breath. This is especially important when working with singers (and also when working with woodwind and brass players), as your up-beat serves as an indication for them to take their preparatory breath.

- When practicing up-beats, you should think about sub-dividing the beat as this will help make sure your up-beat is in the tempo of the music. For example:

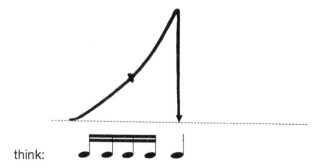

think:

- Make sure that your up-beat leaves from your imaginary beat-line, and that your down-beat lands back on the same imaginary beat-line (not above or below, as this is unclear to follow and will lead to musicians playing ahead or behind the beat).

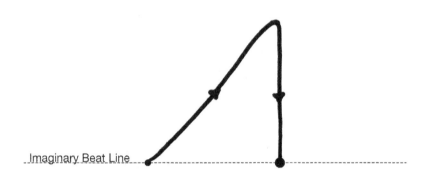

Imaginary Beat Line

CHANGING GEARS

It is rare that all the songs in a show will stay at a constant tempo from beginning to end. You should therefore practice moving the tempo up and down when necessary. If the tempo change is quite dramatic it may become necessary to change the beat pattern accordingly. The exercise below is based around a section of Mozart's *Eine kleine Nachtmusik* and requires you to change beat patterns as the music slows down.

Eine Kleine Nachtmusik: *Allegro*

Composed by Mozart
arranged by S Morley

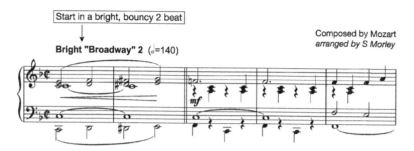

Further Study

Try putting this work in context:

Look at "The Balcony Scene" from "West Side Story" (Leonard Bernstein ♪ / Stephen Sondheim ✎) as an exercise in interchanging between 2, 4 and 8.

This example is excellent for practicing smooth tempo changes, as well as ensuring that you are comfortable interchanging beat patterns and sub-dividing. It has a wide dynamic range so make sure you are reflecting this in your conducting.

Once you have mastered this, try "I am what I am" from "La Cage aux Folles" (Jerry Herman ✎ ♪). This is another example of music which progresses through the different beat patterns and is a good exercise for working on smooth tempo changes.

Work through both examples, initially with a recording so you can familiarize yourself with the vocal line, song structure and orchestration; and then without the recording so the conducting can become second nature. If you have a pianist friend, ask if they will play whilst you conduct to see if what you're beating works in practice.

PAUSES/FERMATAS *(BRITISH/AMERICAN)*

Indicating a pause in the music is relatively straight-forward. The difficulties may arise when we have to indicate when *and how* to leave the pause and continue with the music.

There are three distinct ways to exit a pause. They are as follows:

- "Continuous" – Hold the pause, then give an up-beat into the next beat to move on. There is no break in the music.
- "Off/on" – Hold the pause (on beat 3 for example). To move on – re-give beat 3 as the bring off from the pause and then continue. With an "off-on" (where the "off" to the pause is effectively the up-beat) there will be a break after the pause of one beat.
- "Tramlines" – Hold the pause. Give a clean bring off. When you are ready to move on, give a new up-beat and continue. Here there is a clean break (effectively a pause of silence).

You should practice all of the different types of pauses on each beat of the bar. Here is a written out example of the different types:

Continous Pause

Try to feel like you are drawing out / stretching the beat

Off/On Pause

Tramlines

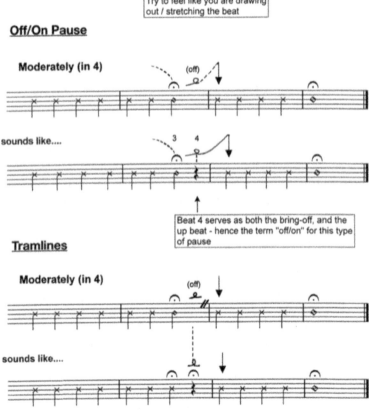

PAUSES IN PRACTICE

Below is a short example containing each of the different types of pauses described above. Try working through the example (ideally in front of a mirror) to ensure you are clear in your conducting delivery.

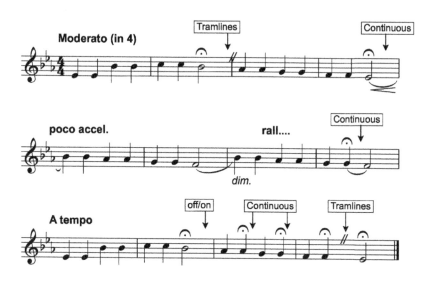

WORKING WITH A BATON

All Musical Directors should be comfortable working with a baton. Sometimes the Actors and Musicians will request you to use one as it makes the beat easier to see in a dark theatre.

There are many different types of baton available, so it is probably best to try some out in your local music shop before making a purchase. You can choose from various shaft lengths (normally 12", 14" or 16"), and from a wide choice of wooden or cork handles. If you are prone to a sweaty palm, it may be advisable to use a cork handle as these absorb the moisture from your hand. A polished wooden handle and a sweaty palm can result in the baton being transformed into a rather lethal javelin if it slips out of your hand in an energized conducting moment!

There are numerous schools of thought on the *correct* way to hold a baton, and one only needs to do a *google* search for pictures of Gergiev, Bernstein and Ashkenazy conducting to see three magnificent conductors holding the baton in three different ways.

For those readers who are unfamiliar with holding a baton, many teachers would agree that the hold advocated by Pierre Monteux is a good hold to adopt.* (Note that the baton should always be held in the right hand.)

- The handle sits in the palm of the hand with the shaft of the baton held between the side of the index finger and the thumb. Take care not to grip the baton too tightly.

Once you have chosen your baton and mastered holding it, you should practice all of the beat patterns with it (in front of the mirror), and practice giving cues so that you can develop your own individual style and technique.

*See the "The Modern Conductor" (Chapter 2) for an in depth discussion on how to hold a baton.

PRACTICING TIPS & HINTS

- The **up-beat** is very important. It is what kick-starts the music. You should always breathe in as you give an up-beat. This helps you focus the beat, and is comparable to the in-breath before singing.

- Try to ensure you **beat line** (the imaginary line that your beat lands on) is in the same place. Practice beating (ideally with a baton – or substitute pencil) on to a surface (using the surface as your beat line). This will help you to find this, and to keep it consistent.

- Make sure your beat has a distinct point at which it lands on the beat line, and don't allow your beat to become too fluid, to the point where there are no defined beats – just pretty arm movements!

- The beat should never stop moving. Avoid sharp bends or kinks in your beat. Always think in curves, and imagine the movements of a bouncing ball when you practice – the point the ball bounces is analogous with your own beat point.

- Think of conducting within different sized boxes. The quieter and more gentle the music, the smaller the box will be. The louder and bigger the music, the larger the box will be.

  Let the size of your box reflect the music you are conducting. Make sure you then stay in your chosen conducting box (avoid the beat going behind your head or over your shoulder as can often happen – this is very unclear and difficult to read/follow).

Small box	Medium Box	Large Box
(quiet, intimate, focused)	*(mezzo forte)*	*(reserved for the big bits!)*

- Avoid any extraneous movements. Often "flowery" and "flamboyant" gestures can creep in because they "look good"! Avoid these, as they only distract from your beat, and can often come across as self-indulgent and surplus to requirements.

- Practice giving clear **shot chords** and **hits**. You will find that the feel of these is all to do with the acceleration of the beat, and it will often feel like the band / orchestra are slightly behind your beat, depending upon your individual style (and on the playing practices of that specific orchestra/ensemble). Try not to let this worry you – as long as they are together as a group is always the most important thing.

Want to practice some shot chords? A good example is the opening of "Greased Lightning" from "Grease" (Jim Jacobs ♪ / Warren Casey ♪) which begins with 3 shot chords.

- When working out the tempo in your mind it is often helpful to think of a **hook line**. This will be a line of the song, or a phrase that instantly gives you the tempo in your head. These lines are often individual to each conductor, and the more experienced you become, the less you will have to think about them, and the whole process will become almost subliminal.

  For example: If we are thinking of the tempo "On the streets where you live" from "My Fair Lady", the line that may instantly jump into your mind could be "Knowing I'm on the streets where you live" (at the end of the song.) If this line is firmly in your mind, and you are thinking of the tempo to start the song (assuming the song in question is going to be a constant tempo throughout of course), then this may be your **hook line**. Therefore if you think of this line before you begin, it will help you to get the tempo for the start of the song.

- If you feel that the band or cast aren't following you, you should resist the urge to make your beat bigger. Bear in mind people may be watching in the peripheral vision and will probably neither register nor respond to a bigger beat. The most effective way to get the band to focus on you is actually to make your beat smaller, and try to make eye contact with the cast/band, encouraging them to focus on your beat.

Practice conducting along to your favourite Original Cast Recordings (sometimes referred to as "OCR"s) in front of a mirror. As well as being a great way to study your technique it is also a great way to learn shows. You will probably pick up tips sub-consciously from some great Musical Directors, as well as absorbing the sounds and styles from the recordings.

PUTTING IT ALL TOGETHER

Take a look at the following example, which is taken from Gilbert & Sullivan's "HMS Pinafore". It is often easiest and clearest to conduct a show from a Piano/Conductor score as opposed to a full orchestral score. If not already indicated, you should take the time to mark in important instrumental cues.

Study the music carefully, then work on the points highlighted in the boxes above the music before trying to conduct the whole number through. Once you have worked through it, try to find some willing musician friends to sing and play for you whilst you conduct. There is no substitute for conducting real people!

- Make a drawing of how you would set up the band pit for this particular show, and imagine the layout in your mind whilst you practice*. Imagine making eye contact with all the players before giving a clear up-beat into the opening bar.

  * The Orchestral Line up for this Operetta is:
  2 Flutes, Oboe, 2 Clarinets, Bassoon,
  2 Horns, 2 Cornets, 2 Trombones,
  Timpani/Percussion,
  Violin 1, Violin 2, Viola, Violoncello, Contrabass

Act 1:No 11 - DUET: "Refrain, Audacious Tar"

JOSEPHINE & RALPH

W.S. Gilbert & Sir Arthur Sullivan
(reduction by S Morley)

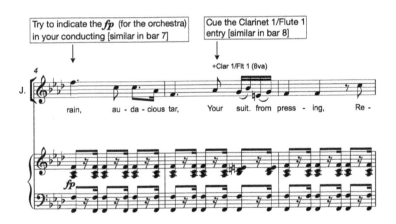

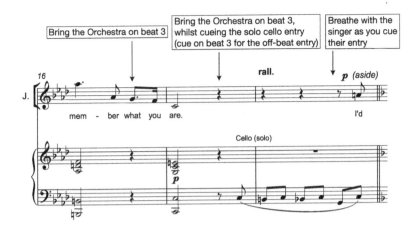

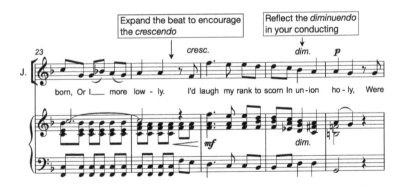

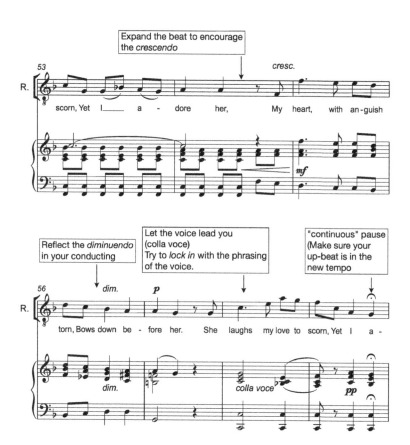

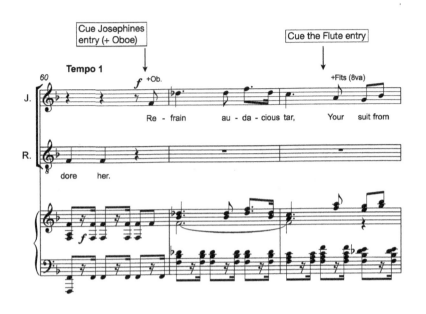

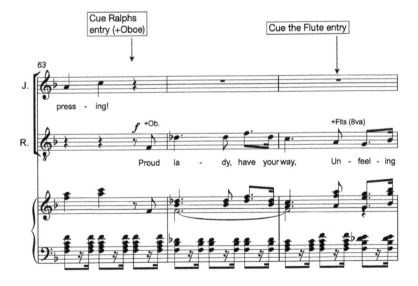

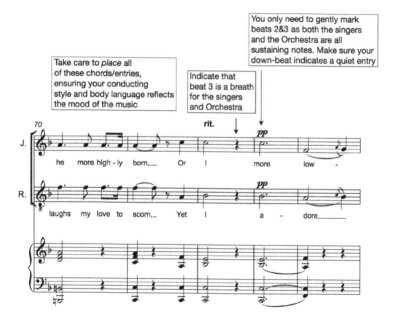

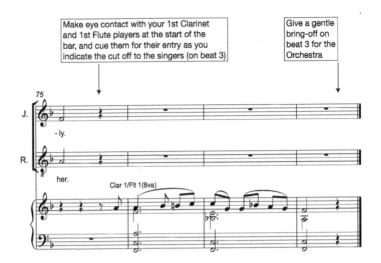

Exit JOSEPHINE, *into cabin*

Appendix 2: **Further Reading**

SUGGESTED VOCAL WARM UP / SINGING BOOKS

Skilbeck, Nicholas / De Mallet Burgess, Thomas
"The Singing and Acting Handbook"
(London: Routledge 2000)

Parkin, Ken
"Anthology of British Tongue-Twisters"
(London: Samuel French 1969)

Brewer, Mike
"Kick Start Your Choir"
(London: Faber Music 1997)

McCallion, Michael
"The Voice Book"
(London, Faber & Faber 1988)

MUSICAL THEATRE AUDITIONS

Mary Hammond (with Emer Gillespie & Nigel Lilley)
"Thank you – that's all we need for today…"
(London, Edition Peters 2009)

SUGGESTED CONDUCTING TECHNIQUE BOOKS/DVDs

McElheran, Brock
"Conducting Technique – for Beginners and Professionals"
(New York & Oxford: Oxford University Press 1989)

Lumley, John / Springthorpe, Nigel
"The Art of Conducting"
(London: Rhinegold Publishing Ltd 1989)

Green, Elizabeth A.H. / Gibson, Mark
"The Modern Conductor"
Prentice Hall, 2004

"Art of Conducting – Great Conductors of the Past" (DVD)
(Teldec Video – Warner Classics 2002)

ACCENT & PHONETICS BOOKS/CDS

Robert Blumenfeld
"Accents: A Manual for Actors"
(Limelight Editions 2002)

Penny Dyer and Gwyneth Strong
"Access Accents (Performance Books): An Accent Training Resource for Actors"
 RP & General American
[Audiobook & Audio CD]
(Methuen Drama 2007)

Peter Roach
"Phonetics"
(OUP 2001)

HISTORY OF MUSICALS & HISTORY OF MUSICAL THEATRE BOOKS/DVDS/CDS

Bordman, Gerald & Norton, Richard
"American Musical Theatre – A Chronicle"
(USA: Oxford University Press, 2011)

Hirschak, Thomas S.
"The Oxford Companion to the American Musical"
(USA: Oxford University Press, 2008)

Gänzl, Kurt
"Musicals"
(London: Carlton Books Ltd 2001)

Evans, Mike
"Musicals – Facts, Figures and Fun"
(London: AAPPL Artists' and Photographers' Press Ltd 2006)

Bering, Rüdiger
"Musicals – An illustrated historical overview"
(New York: Barron's Educational Series, Inc. 1997)

Fawkes, Richard
"The History of the Musical" (Audiobook – CD)
(England: Naxos AudioBooks 2001)

Fields, Marc / Kantor, Michael
"The History of Broadway" (DVD)
(ITV DVD 2005)

BOOKS ON SOUND / SOUND DESIGN

White, Paul
"Basic Live Sound"
(London: Sanctuary Publishing Ltd. 2000)

BOOKS ABOUT ORCHESTRATION

Riddle, Nelson
"*Arranged* by Nelson Riddle"
(Alfred, 1985)

Mancini, Henry
"Sounds and Scores"
(Music Sales, Ltd New edition 1997)

Piston, Walter
"Orchestration"
(W.W. Norton & Co., 1955)

Forsyth, Cecil
"Orchestration"
(Dover, New Edition1986)

LIST OF MUSICAL EXAMPLES

Eine Kleine Nachtmusik (Allegro) – Composed by W.A Mozart
Arranged by Stuart Morley

"Flash" – Words & Music by Brian May
Used by kind permission

"Refrain, Audatious Tar" from *HMS Pinafore*
Music by Sir Arthur Sullivan, Lyrics by WS Gilbert
Piano Reduction by Stuart Morley

"Merano" from *Chess*
Written by Sir Tim Rice, Benny Andersson & Björn Ulvaeus
(Copyright: Wise Publications) *Used by kind permission*

"Merrie England" from *Merrie England*
Written by Basil Hood, Music by Edward German

"Listening to you" from *Tommy*
Music & Lyrics by Pete Townshend
© 1969 Fabulous Music Ltd.
Suite 2.07, Plaza 535 Kings Road, London SW10 0SZ
International Copyright Secured.
All Rights Reserved. Used by Permission.

EDITED BY
SIMON MORLEY BSc (Hons) MRPharmS

PHOTOGRAPHY BY
LIZZIE OTTLEY
All rights reserved

Special thanks to Tom King for modelling the Comms headset and pack.

Acknowledgements

Thanks to all my teachers, mentors and friends for their help and inspiration:

Stuart & Irene Atkinson, James Adler, Kevin Amos, Stuart Barr, Stephen Brooker, Ray Cooney, Rob Cousins, Marc Day and all at the Millfield Theatre, Mike Dixon, Neil Drinkwater, Tony Edge, David Firman, Chris Fisher, George Hall, Mary Hammond, Stephen Hill, Norm Hirschy, Steve Holness, Dave Howson, Laurie and Mike, Richy Machin, Brian May, Ruth Massey, MYT, June Nobbs, Mark & Jane Nuti, Cy Payne, Simon Pickering, David Putsey, Karen Rabinovitz, Andy Read, Steph Reeve, Sir Tim Rice, Greg Rose, Maureen Scott, Donald Simpson, Nick Skilbeck, Anne Marie Speed, David Steadman, Keith Strachan, Clive Swift, Corinne Vallé, Chris & Annie Walker, Mark Warman, David White, Douglas Whyte, Hugh Wooldridge, Pete Woollard and to all of the fantastic musicians I have been lucky enough to work with.

Thanks to Tony, Georgia, Peter, Chris and all at the Dominion.

Thanks to Fabulous Music, Brian May & Tim Rice for allowing me to use their music and lyrics as examples.

Special thanks to Simon for proofreading and editing the Handbook.

Special thanks to Ben Elton for kindly agreeing to write the Foreword.

Extra special thanks to Lizzie, Mum & Dad, Si, Katie & Gracie, Sharon, Mark & Josh, and Ieu for all their love, support, encouragement and endurance!

A

Accents, 57, 60
Accompanist, 35
Accompanying, 35
Actor, 9
Actor - Musical Director, 60
Actor/muso, 10
Adults (working with), 150
Ambidextral brain teasers, 44
Ambidextrous conductor, 43
Artistic Team, 2, 117
Aspirate Onset, 54
Audition notes, 96
Audition Pianists, 97
Audition Process, 94
Audition schedule, 98
Auditions, 93
Aural Skills, 58

B

Back Line, 66
Back stage calls, 142
Backing Tracks, 154
Baton, 181
Beat Patterns, 167
Beethoven's 5ᵗ Symphony, 24
Bel Canto, 53
Belting, 52
Breathing, 77
Busk, 37

C

Chest Voice, 53
Children (working with), 149
Choir, 60
Choreographers, 118
Clavicular breathing, 54, 55
Click Tracks, 67
Comms, 45
Conduct from the keyboard, 43
Conducting a Run, 146
Conducting Shorthand, 90

Conductor, 8, 15
Copyist, 65
Count-ins, 91
Creek Onset, 54
Cue light system, 46
Cue Lights, 45
Cue Lines, 86
Cue on an off-beat, 24
Cues, 21
Cues on different beats, 22
CV/Resume, 163

D

Dancers, 118
Dancers counts, 119
Dance knowledge, 122
Deputy Stage Manager, 45
DI Box, 66
Dictaphone or digital voice
    recorder, 109
Diction & Pronunciation, 74
Dress Rehearsal, 141

E

Ear Training, 37
Effects, 66
EQ, 67
Estill Voice Technique, 52

F

Falsetto, 53
Fermatas, 179
First Rehearsal, 101
Flash, 29
Foldback, 67
Front of House (FOH), 67

G

Giving Notes, 143
Glottal Onset, 54
Groove, 41

T

U

V

W

X

Y

CPSIA information can be obtained at www.ICGtesting.com
Printed in the USA
BVOW11s1950290514

354710BV00009B/611/P